Totally

Totally

An Insider's Look at the Crazy World of BBQ

George Hensler

Published by Foodways Editions,
an Imprint of Sunbelt Media

Dedication

For David Robert Knox,
October 5, 1986- October 16, 2006
Friend, cousin, nephew, brother, son, grandson,
you are forever in our hearts.

Totally Q

Contents

Totally Q

Acknowledgements

Many people were instrumental in supplying valuable information, assistance or direction for this book and for that I am very grateful. I would like to acknowledge and thank the following folks for their helpful contributions: Carolyn Wells, Bob Sammons, Dan Hixon, Ardie Davis, Craig 'Meathead' Goldwyn, Melissa Pate, Harry Soo, Scotty Johnson, Bruce Tindall, Kelly Cain, Randy Mcgee, and Lois Manno.

I would also like to add a very special thanks and tip of the hat to Dave DeWitt, aka "The Pope of Peppers," for generating the idea for this project. His assistance, advice and encouragement have been invaluable during the process. Thanks, Dave!

Barbecue: The Meaning of the Word

Barbecue, barbque, BB-Q, bar-B-Q, 'cue, BBQ, bar-be-que, barbie-q, barbeque, BB-Que, barbacoa, bar-b-que,'Que, barbicue, barbique, bar-b-cue, or just plain old Q

Which spelling is correct? Is it a noun or a verb? Am I hosting a barbecue or a cook-out? Is it grilling, smoking or barbequing?

I will further illustrate the confusion of trying to sort out these meanings by using the word(s) in a paragraph, which I am sure after reading, will cause you to run screaming into the night: *I am going down to Archie's BBQ Restaurant to eat some of his barbecue chicken that he bar-b-ques on his father's old time barbeque pit. I tell you, that guy has some of the best barbecue around. The best part is when he slathers on that delicious BBQ sauce just before he takes that barbecue off the barbeque. He serves his delicious BBQ up with some real good barbecue sauce, and the whole meal is served in full view of that old-time barbeque pit.*

Stop the ride, I want to get off! I have fallen and I can't get up! I have spent at least two days researching, head scratching, reading, looking, screaming, laughing and crying, all while trying to sort out the discrepancies, disagreements, definitions and discussions on these very meaty questions.

To get a more in-depth idea of what I'm talking about, one need only Google "the difference between barbecue and grilling" and start sifting through the 1,470,000 hits that result. A search for "the difference between barbecue and BBQ" yields fewer hits, only 1,350,000, and I haven't even begun to plug in the numerous spelling variations that currently populate our vernacular. Even the spell check function on my MS Word computer program cannot offer a definitive answer, allowing spellings of both barbecue and barbeque as correct. My head hurts.

When I made my last query regarding the difference between barbecue and BBQ, I found this reply on Answers.com: *The spelling* barbeque—*with que at the end—comes*

Totally Q

from combining the standard spelling barbecue *with the abbreviation* Bar-B-Q, *and from spelling as you speak. Though listed as an alternative in some dictionaries,* barbeque *is best avoided.*

This really cleared things up for me, although after reading this definition and then reaching over for another slug of wine (an essential beverage when conducting research on a topic such as this), I wondered aloud if the writer thought that barbeque in general, "is best when avoided." I had to hope he did not.

Although I am not quite sure that I would recommend looking to our politicians and bureaucrats for any clarification on this topic, which many of us " smoke fiends" hold near and dear to our hearts, several times during my quest, I stumbled upon the following definition supplied by our dear ol' Uncle Sam. No, this is not the crazy uncle that every family has, but no one wants to talk about; I am talking about the federal government here and any similarities to anyone's crazy Uncle Sam are purely unintentional, with deference given to the crazy uncle.

According to the Code of Federal Regulations, Title 9, Chapter III, Part 319, Subpart C, Section 319.80, revised in 1985: "Barbecued meats, such as product labeled 'Beef Barbecue' or 'Barbecued Pork' shall be cooked by the direct action of dry heat resulting from the burning of hard wood or the hot coals there from for a sufficient period to assume the usual characteristics of a barbecued article, which include the formation of a brown crust on the surface and the rendering of surface fat. The product may be basted with a sauce during the cooking process. The weight of barbecued meat shall not exceed 70 percent of the weight of the fresh uncooked meat."

Seems that every time I thought I had THE answer, I found yet another opinion or definition to confuse the issue, and the more I thought about it, the more I realized that we've been over thinking the entire thing. It doesn't help matters, either, when certain single-minded "our way or the highway" factions or groups look down their smoke-filled nostrils at other folks who want to be a part of the club, but have different opinions or ideas.

Cliques, clubs, groups and forums have been formed, all with (supposedly) the same goal in mind. However, just like an onion, the more you peel it, the more layers you find. The charcoal folks look at the gas cooker folks as if they were from another country, while the stick burners think they are the only true pitmasters. Bring up the topic of electric temperature control devices to some purists and they look at you as if you had three heads.

Totally Q

The sad part about all of this petty bickering is that we are all supposed to be on the same team, aren't we? We all enjoy good food, a few cool drinks, some nice tunes, and the company of our friends and families, along with the sounds and smells associated with outdoor cooking. Can't we all just get along?

And so, in the interest of diplomatic relations and barbecue unity, it is by the power vested in me by the North American Chapter of WTHDBBQMTM, (What The Heck Does BBQ Mean To Me), that I hereby announce and further decree the definitive meaning and definition:

Going forward, there will be no issue as to the meaning and or use of the words barbecue, BBQ, barbeque, bar-b-que or any other variation or combination of these letters or words. For purposes of this declaration, the word "barbecue" will be used as an encompassing and inclusive designation for the numerous flavors, techniques, equipment and fuel sources used for smoking, grilling or pit-cooking any variety of meats. This is done with complete acknowledgment that any and all derivations of this word or combination of letters are all completely interchangeable and have no immediate effect on the ultimate meanings, uses or definitions.

By the way, for informational, legal, and factual reasons, I feel I must tell you that the North American Chapter of WTHDBBQMTM is strictly a figment of my warped, and at times, demented imagination. Any similarity to anyone one or anything either living or dead is purely accidental and unintentional.

One Word, Many Meanings

Barbecue *(verb)*: A method of cooking. Can include—but is not limited to—slow roasting, pit cooking (above- and below-ground), slow cooking, grilling, (conventional?) smoking, hot and fast smoking, wrapping in wet leaves and spit cooking. The heat or fuel source does not matter: charcoal, wood, gas, electricity, and pellets are all acceptable.

Barbecue *(noun)*: 1) A cooking device or vessel used to accomplish any of the previously-defined cooking methods. Can be made of steel, iron, tin, stainless, brick, aluminum, concrete, wood, ceramic or glass and used with a variety of heat sources 2) Food prepared with any of the previously-named devices and methods. 3) A gathering or event where food prepared with any "barbecue" method or device is served, along with copious amounts of ice cold adult beverages. 4) A joint or establishment where folks congregate to enjoy food prepared using any of the aforementioned procedures and equipment. In other words, a restaurant.

3

Totally Q

Photo courtesy of Sunbelt Archives

Barbecue *(adjective)*: Used to describe the flavor or taste of any product seasoned with barbecue flavors, as in BBQ potato chips.

In addition, you will see the following abbreviations used informally throughout this book:

BBQ *(noun)*: Popular synonym for *barbecue.*

'Cue *(noun)*: Slang term for barbecue among competition cooks. Other forms include 'que and 'Q.

'Cueology *(noun)*: Slang term meaning the science and techniques of barbecue.

There, that ought to clear things up, right? The bottom line here, and borrowing from a worn out cliché, is this: It's all good. We should all be one big happy family. An e-mail I received from my friend Craig "Meathead" Goldwyn, creator of the super website www.amazingribs.com, underscores this sentiment by pointing out that there's no one "right" way to barbecue. *"For the past 10-20 years,"* he said, *"we have been turning up our noses at backyard cooks and telling them, 'That's not barbecue, that's grilling.' Well I say that's snobbery, and it is technically, factually incorrect."*

Ardie Davis (a.k.a. Remus Powers) takes this stance a step further in the July 2010 edition of the *National Barbecue News* with a call for wider acceptance: "Why, when there are millions of backyard cooks in America, do we have fewer than a million subscribers to the *National Barbecue News?* Why does the world's largest barbecue organization have only 13,000+ members? There are surely many reasons, but let's not let one of the reasons be ourselves. Backyard cooking with wood fires, charcoal, solar power or gas is a gateway to our network. Let's open wide the gate, unfurl the red carpet, and welcome all backyard cooks and others to our fold!"

Ardie makes a great point here and sums it up better than anyone in saying, *"Let's celebrate barbecue in all its manifestations. Let's welcome the millions who should be among us but don't know they are welcome!"*

Well said Ardie, let me help you open the door.

The Etymology of Barbecue
According to barbecue history buff Laura Dove, "The most plausible theory states that the word *barbecue* is a derivative of the West Indian term *barbacoa*, which denotes a method of slow-cooking meat over hot coals. *Bon Appetit* Magazine blithely informs its readers that the word comes from an extinct tribe in Guyana that enjoyed "cheerfully spit roasting captured enemies." *The Oxford English Dictionary* traces the word back to Haiti, and others claim (somewhat implausibly) that *barbecue* actually comes from the French phrase *barbe a queue*, meaning *from head to tail*. Proponents of this theory point to the whole-hog cooking method espoused by some barbecue chefs. *Tar Heel* magazine posits that the word *barbecue* comes from a 19th century advertisement for a combination whiskey bar, beer hall, pool establishment and purveyor of roast pig, known as the BAR-BEER-CUE-PIG. The most convincing explanation is that the method of roasting meat over powdery coals was picked up from indigenous peoples in the Colonial period, and that *barbacoa* became barbecue in the lexicon of early settlers."

And Still Another Theory
As I am sure you are aware, much discussion has been held as to the origin of the word *barbecue*. It seems like everywhere you go, someone has a thought or opinion as to where it all began and not to be outdone, the folks in Texas have their own theory as to the beginnings of the word. According to legend, there was a Texan named Barnaby Quinn, or perhaps his name was Bernard Quayle. Either way, his initials are BQ, which is the important thing here. Now, this fellow liked to throw large parties and cook whole animals over big open pits. As the word *barbecue* hadn't been invented yet, I am not quite sure what these gatherings were called perhaps "bull roasts," if in fact a whole cow happened to be spinning on the spit, but I will leave this discussion for another day.

The important part is that this rancher used a branding iron to mark his livestock, as did most of the other ranchers in Texas, except this guy's branding iron had his initials

Totally Q

with a line underneath, as in BQ. Ranches around those parts were named after their brand, and I am told that a straight line is called a "bar." Thus, Bar-B-Q was born, at least according to the folks from Texas anyway, thank you Bernie or Barby. Hey, maybe this is why the folks in Australia started called their grills *barbies*...I think further investigation is needed here.

Trigrammawhatsis?

"Consider the mystic Trigrammaton, BBQ. It is not in itself a word. Nor is it an acronym. It is rarely sounded out, like TVA, NBC, or BBC. Usually it is pronounced barbecue just as X-mas is pronounced Christmas. Which means linguistically speaking, it is an abbreviation."—*Holy Smoke, The Big Book of North Carolina Barbecue* by John Shelton Reed and Dale Volberg Reed

Whip it Good

While interpreting a book written in 1798, a French translator attempted to explain the word *barbacue* [sic]: "This barbarous amusement consists of whipping hogs almost to death to make the flesh more delicate. I do not know that even cannibals practice it." Now, I am not saying the French are arrogant; you can be the judge of that. What I want to know is: *Does this really work?*

Worshiping at the Altar of 'Que

"Barbecue is like religion: First, because it can make you swoon in jubilation; and second, because it has so many different sects. There are true believers who are convinced that their kind of barbecue is the *only* good and true one, and that people who use an unorthodox type of wood for their fire, or make sauce a little differently, are heretics." –Food writers Jane and Michael Stern

"Barbecue is a taste of the South. It's a noun, a verb, and an entire religion served on a bun...Roll up your sleeves, grab a pile of napkins, and wait for manna from heaven." —Author Michael Lee West

"A primitive summertime rite at which spirits are present, hunks of meat are sacrificed by being burnt on braziers by sauce-smeared men wearing old hats and aprons with cabalistic slogans, and human flesh is offered to insects." —Humorist and author Henry Beard

"Barbecue, therefore, is at the core of modern civilization. It tames wild men and completes the hearts of heroes. It's not just a way to kill a Sunday afternoon; it's the heart of the world's oldest religion, which will guide you in a balanced life." —*The Man's Book of the BBQ* by Brendan McGinley

Totally Q

An Early BBQ Snob

In what is perhaps the earliest official sighting of that not-so-rare bird known as the Barbecue Snob, Rufus Jarman wrote this in a 1954 issue of *The Saturday Evening Post:* "Nowadays, barbecuing, or something so called, has spread throughout the land. These days it isn't politics so much as the popularity of back-yard cookery that promotes barbecuing. Countless men in chef's caps and fancy aprons, with their eyes reddened by smoke, regale their guests with burnt and raw flesh. Many Georgia epicures insist that this is an insult to the honorable name of barbecue. They assert that, statements in various magazines to the contrary, you cannot barbecue hamburgers, roasting ears, potatoes, onions, tomatoes, wieners or salami, and it is a shame and disgrace to mention barbecuing in connection with such foolishness."

Them's Spittin' Words

"Many of our familiar grilled-meat dishes," wrote Elisabeth Rozin, food historian and cookbook author, "have their origin in the Middle East and Central Asia, and involve meat, usually lamb, marinated in oil and spices, then spitted and cooked over hot coals. *Shish kabob* comes from the Turkish word *shish (pronounced sis)* which means *skewer* and *kabob (kebab, kebap)* means a *chunk of meat.* In Russian, the dish is called *shashlik,* and in Greek *souvlakia.* It is interesting that both *grill* and *skewer* have additionally entered our contemporary vocabulary as unabashedly aggressive metaphors: to 'grill' someone means to question relentlessly, to subject him to heat; to 'skewer' means to puncture, to defeat, to nail someone to the wall."

Outdoor Cooking—The Gateway Drug

Author Betty Wason blamed barbecue for the inevitable blurring of gender-specific activities like cooking. "It was the popularity of outdoor barbecues that led most American husbands to take an interest in cookery. While the kitchen had come to be regarded as the woman's sphere from frontier days onward, cooking out of doors was different. It reminded grown men of Boy Scout days when they roasted hot dogs over campfires. Building up the fire in the charcoal grill was thoroughly masculine. So was the cooking of a steak. Before long, the barbecue cooks were adding sauces to their outdoor masterpieces and,

The fun doesn't stop just because the sun goes down at a BBQ contest. Photo by George Hensler.

Totally Q

once caught by the spell of creative cooking, began to launch into intricate and unusual dishes." I guess you could say 'cue appeals to all us Boy Scouts who don't want to grow up!

It's a Man Thang

"I'm a man. Men cook outside. Women make the three-bean salad. That's the way it is and always has been, since the first settlers of Levittown. That outdoor grilling is a manly pursuit has long been beyond question. If this wasn't firmly understood, you'd never get grown men to put on those aprons with pictures of dancing wienies and things on the front, and messages like *Come N' Get It!* Some men wear little chef's hats, too, accessorized with big padded barbecue gloves. They wear them willingly, without a whimper. Try putting that stuff on the family dog."—Author and journalist Bill Geist

The Many Faces of 'Que

Hailed by the *Wall Street Journal* as "one of gastronomy's first citizens," food writer Jeffrey Steingarten described the many manifestations of 'cue across America: "Real barbecue is one of the most delicious foods ever devised by humankind. But it takes on varying forms and shapes. In Memphis, a pork barbecue sandwich consists of pulled (or pulled and then chopped) shoulder on a hamburger bun, doused with a tomato-based sauce that is tangy, mildly sweet, and barely piquant—and topped with a scoop of coleslaw. In Kentucky, pork becomes mutton. In North Carolina, the mild tanginess of Tennessee becomes the powerful force of vinegar, and in South Carolina the tomato-based sauce is replaced by mustard. Drive 100 miles into Missouri,

The author (second from right) with his competition BBQ Team, "Who Are Those Guys?"
Photo courtesy of George Hensler

and the whole pork shoulder yields to the smaller butt portion. If you travel further west than Arkansas, pork gives way to beef and poultry."

What's a Ribfest?

The word *ribfest* is actually a shortened version of *rib festival*. These rib cook-offs are held each year all across North America and feature teams of cooks, sometimes known as "ribbers," who travel from every part of the continent to compete and vend at these very popular events. Many times, the winner will be chosen by a "People's Choice" method and often the festival also highlights various musical performers. One of the largest ribfests is held each September on the shores of Lake Ontario in Burlington, Ontario, which attracts over 175,000 rib connoisseurs during its four-day run.

Burnt Ends

"If barbecue were an argument, it'd be a beer brawl. Barbecue fanatics debate it, dissect it, discuss it, analyze it, judge it, go on expeditions in search of some of the best plates of it, celebrate it, scorn the pretenders of it, and finally, they eat it. And they do all of this with sanctimony, belligerence, or both." —Jim Shahin

"*Barbacoa,* beginning life as a Caribbean noun for cooking and other frames, thus morphed into the English barbecue as a result of a complex and confusing etymology." —Andrew Warnes

"A process whereby a large cut of tough meat is cooked by the smoke of a hardwood fire at low temperatures (210 degrees or less) for a long period of time, with doneness determined by the meat's tenderness." —Chris Schlesinger

"True barbecue, let me explain, is meat slow-roasted over wood at a low enough temperature to lose about a third of its weight in moisture during the cooking process." —John Thorne

"Barbecue is the quintessential American food, perhaps the only one large enough to reconcile the myths out of which the fabric of our national truth has been woven. Barbecue, then, serves as a metaphor for American culture, bridging and embracing this nation's various facets."—Lolis Eric Elie

"Barbecue can be a verb or a noun. It can mean pulled pork or beef ribs. And, especially in the American South, it can cause intense debate and stir regional pride." —Andrew Warnes

Totally Q

"Barbecue is more than just a cooking method in America. It's a noun, a verb, and a part of the social culture in some parts of the country."
—Author and Pitmaster Rick Browne, Ph.B.

"What do I like the most [about barbecue]? The eating, man! And besides, I get to play with fire and smoke every day. How many people get to say that? There is something primal about cooking meat with fire. Mastering the elements and producing something delicious. I think that just strikes a chord in all of us."
—Neil "Bigmista" Strawder- Bigmista's BBQ

"And while I hate to dispute American excellence in anything, I have to disclose that just about everyone on the planet grills, barbecues, smokes, or cooks food outdoors. Barbecue is, in fact, a universal language."—Author and Pitmaster Rick Browne, Ph.B.

A typical cookoff day at the American Royal. This was from 2003.
Photo by Mike Stines, courtesy of Sunbelt Archives

The Evolution
of Barbecue

A s a kid growing up in the early 60s just outside of Baltimore in Essex, Maryland, my first memories of outdoor cooking were summer holiday gatherings
in our back yard. Memorial Day usually kicked off the "grilling season."
When my father broke out the familiar red, white, and blue bag of Kingsford charcoal and whatever brand of lighter fluid that happened to be lying around from the
last season.

He would drag out the grill, which had been under the porch since the previous
Labor Day, and dump out any water that had accumulated, along with the remnants of charcoal. After the grill grate was removed, my brother Tom or I would be
assigned cleaning duties. This usually resulted in a spirited discussion as to who had
last completed the unpleasant task the last time the duty presented itself. The conversation was then more than likely cut short by my father's suggestion that unless either
one of us was in the mood for some lower posterior shoe removal, we should get the
grill scrubbed off and quit the arguing.

I feel I need to back up a minute here to talk about the grill itself...I'm not sure who
made the unit, but if my fading memory is even somewhat correct, almost everyone
in the neighborhood had the same type: A round, open-type deal with three 3 legs
and two wheels that sometimes fell off while maneuvering. The grill grate had a long
rod in the center that fed down into a sleeve, under which was a lever-type setup that
adjusted the distance between the food and the heat. This usually worked when the
unit was new, but its effectiveness seemed to fall away with age and neglect.

When everything was cleaned up, Dad would tear off a clean sheet of aluminum foil,
which he placed into the bottom of the grill chamber, followed by added a shovelful
or two of sand as a bed for the charcoal. The reasoning, I was told, was to absorb
the grease. We then loaded in a fairly generous pile of briquettes, which had to be
arranged in just the right way by the resident pitmaster, Dad. He then added a few
healthy squirts of charcoal lighter fluid and told us to stand back before he struck the

Totally Q

match. I'll never forget that smell, which usually meant that family and friends were coming and we were all in for a treat.

As I think back now I ask myself: *Is it any wonder we only grilled out a few times a year? This was way too much work!* I'm guessing our family back then was like many others around the country. Dad worked all day climbing poles for the phone company, came home to a dinner my mother had prepared, read the paper, watched the evening news on the single TV in the house, fell asleep for a while in the chair, went to bed, then got up the next day and did it all over again. There just wasn't any time or interest in outdoor cooking except for occasional holidays and weekends.

Fast forward to 2012. With the increased ease and popularity of gas grills, families are cooking out year-round and manufacturers have taken the outdoor cooking experience to levels never before seen. In addition, numerous fuel sources are more conveniently available than ever. In the 60s we used whatever brand of charcoal was sold in the hardware store down the street, but today's home centers have entire sections devoted to outdoor cooking products and offer not only several types of charcoal, but also a wide selection of woods for smoking.

As is typical in modern-day America, we continue to push the envelope. Outdoor kitchen arenas, complete with wood-fired ovens, table-mounted cookers and grills, running water, stereo sound, and even granite counter tops, are becoming more prevalent. Cable television beams numerous food and cooking shows 24/7 and their

From basic equipment like this, magic is made...if the wizard knows what he (or she) is doing, that is. Photo courtesy of Sunbelt Archives.

success has allowed many of the personalities from these programs to become huge stars in their own rights. Cooking contests—particularly competition barbecue—have seen a huge increase in popularity among both participants and spectators, due in no small part to what we have seen on television. The TLC show *BBQ Pitmasters* is a prime example.

From its humble beginnings with prehistoric man, the world of barbecue has surely come a long way in a relatively short time, with significant advances in the last 30 years or so. While we don't know what the future holds, we definitely have some ideas about the events and inventions that have influenced the evolution of this rustic—yet refined—cusine, some of which are highlighted in the following section.

An Unofficial
Barbecued Timeline

1.5 million years ago: Scientists believe that early man began to walk in a more upright stature so that he could follow herds of animals over long distances. It is thought by many that while following these herds, man began to dream of the various spices and sauces he would use to cover the beast, should he ever be fortunate enough to capture and slay one.

600,000 years ago: It is reported that the species *homo heidelbergensis* left footprints in powdered material that scientists claim was volcanic ash. Recent studies, however, have determined that the substance was actually residue from charcoal, and could very well be evidence of early cookouts.

200,000-400,000 years ago: Man discovered fire. While this certainly is a wide time range and there is a good amount of discussion on this topic, it's safe to assume that shortly after this discovery was made, man, even in his earliest form, was well on the way to braising some prehistoric beast using the low and slow method of cooking. Even then, no one could dispute the fact that cooked meat tastes a whole lot better than raw meat.

160,000 years ago: According to evidence found in fossilized form, it's speculated that *Homo sapiens* in Ethiopia were butchering hippos as a part of some type of mortuary ritual, providing further evidence that barbecue was present in the Stone Age.

10,000-40,000 years ago: What modern-day paleontologists are now dubbing "'cue-magnon man" was alleged to have existed during the Upper Paleolithic period. Scientists have stumbled upon a likely rudimentary cook site in Asia, evidenced by remnants of charcoal, animal bones and some type of a crude brush or mopping

Totally Q

device. Flask-like vessels were found in the area, some of which appear to have contained a type of fermented fruit juice or ale product. Scientists also discovered what appears to be a statue carved into the shape of a prehistoric swine-like creature. This gives credence to recent hypotheses that the modern-day barbecue contest descended from our prehistoric ancestors.

6,000-7,000 years ago: The Mesolithic Age ended. Man had developed more efficient hunting tools, built more complex settlements and the Neolithic cultures developed large-scale agriculture in the fertile valleys of the Middle East. Some say this area was a natural for growing large, full heads of cabbage and was possibly the homeland of cole slaw, as well as many of the other side dishes known to accompany slow-cooked meat products.

6,000 years ago: The Emperor of China, by royal decree, ordered all of his subjects to raise and breed hogs. I am guessing the Emp himself was a real bacon/pulled pork lover, and I'll bet he cooked his 'cue in a Big Green Egg.

5,000 years ago: Fred Flintstone and his pal Barney Rubble made prehistoric barbecue history when they ordered a slab of ribs so big it caused Fred's sedan to tip over. This was quite a feat, when you consider the tires on Fred's jalopy were made of solid stone. Due to their ensuing popularity, the modern stone-age family made "brontosaurus burger" a household word.

4,600 years ago: Evidence of a tall, urn-shaped, clay cooking device fueled by charcoal was found in Rajasthan, India by anthropologists. Some say this was one of the first known grills or barbecue cookers.

3,800 years ago: The *Epic of Gilgamesh* is considered one of the earliest known surviving works of literature and is a poem traced back to Mesopotamia. My research finds several barbecue references here. In *Tablet Six*, Enkidu and Gilgamesh slay the "bull of heaven," and offer its heart to Shamash, but when a hep-cat named Ishtar complains (I have never been a huge "organ" fan myself), Enkidu chucks a hindquarter at him. It's my best guess that ol' Ishtar picked up the "chucked" roast and took it immediately to the nearest fire, possibly explaining the origin for the term "chuck" roast. Further support for my half-baked theory comes in *Tablet Eight*, which states that, "A great banquet is held where the treasures are offered to the gods of the Netherworld." Sure sounds like a barbecue to me.

251 A.D.: Bishop Alexander of Comana was burned to death. Known as the Patron Saint of Charcoal, his official feast day is August 11, during high barbecue season.

1248: What would later be determined as the forerunner of various grilling and smoking associations like KCBS, Les Oyers, the Goose Roasters Guild, was founded in Paris, France. In 1509, the organization's name was changed to Les Rotisseurs and is considered to have been the first professional organization for grillmeisters.

1320: The renowned medieval chef Guillaume Tirel was born. His famous cookbook, titled *Le Viandier*, included recipes for grilling crane, swan and peacock.

1360: A Frenchman named Henry de Vick invented a mechanical clock. Chefs in the area then adapted the turning mechanisms for rudimentary motorized spits or rotisseries for grilling meats. It's my guess that some of these chefs were the early descendants of Rube Goldberg.

1487: Thought by some hot dog aficionados to be the year the frankfurter was developed in—where else? Frankfurt, Germany!

1492: Christopher Columbus makes a wrong turn and discovers the Bahamas and West Indies. While he is ashore asking for directions, he collects some chile peppers, which are later used to spice up the drab barbecue sauces made by his ship's cooks.

1516: Spaniard Gonzalo Fernandez de Oviedo y Valdes is the first known European to describe a *barbacoa*, a wooden grill-type structure built over a fire, that was used by the Taíno Indians of the Caribbean.

1539: Spanish explorer Hermando DeSoto first introduced pigs to the continent of North America.

1540: On March 25 of this year, DeSoto and about 40 of his fellow pillage and plunderers invaded a village located in what is now known as the state of Georgia, where they found venison and whole turkeys smoking on a *barbacoa*. Some historians contend this was one of the first barbecues recorded by Europeans in the New World.

1557: The word *barbacoa* appears in the colonial writings of German adventurer and conquistador Nikolaus Federmann.

1580: An engraving dated back to this century shows several American Indians using a grill-like device to cook and smoke fish.

1598: On April 30, the territory of Texas saw one of its first large-scale barbecues. It was held on the Rio Grande near San Elizario, which is located about 30 miles from El Paso. The menu that day featured roasted wild game, roasted veggies, hard biscuits, salt pork and red wine.

1607: Sir Walter Raleigh first brought pigs to the colony of Jamestown, Virginia.

1610: According to the book *Real Barbecue*, the first known mention of the word *barbecue* in the New World was found in the House of Virginia Burgesses, where a law was recorded that forbade "the shooting of firearms for sport at barbecues, else how shall we know when the Indians are coming?"

1611: The Pilgrims first brought cows to North America.

1655: According to some, the word *barbecue* first appeared in print in the *Dictionary of American English*.

1666: In what would later be known as one of the first travel brochures, residents of the soon-to-be state of North Carolina had a flyer printed to entice British immigrants to their settlement. They claimed the area was prime habitat for raising hogs due to the abundance of acorns and other browse.

1707: An Englishman by the name of Edward Ward mentions a barbecue feast in a journal called the *London Spy*. This satirical writer titled his piece *The Barbacue Feast: Or, the Three Pigs of Peckham, Broil'd Under an Apple-tree*.

1727: One of the first recipes for catsup was printed in Elizabeth Smith's *Complete Housewife*. The concoction is thought to be a forerunner of barbecue sauce.

1732: *The Country Housewife and the Lady's Director in the Management of a House, and the Delights and Profits of a Farm*, an early cookbook by R. Bradley, included instructions on how to prepare a whole hog for the pit.

1733: The poet Alexander Pope wrote that some guy named Oldfield (who could really pack away the groceries) was alleged to have said, "Send me Gods! A whole hog barbecu'd! [sic] ."

1738: George Washington, the Father of Our Country, is alleged to have chopped down the now famous cherry tree. We can only surmise that he was collecting wood chips for his smoker.

1750: A swamp located in Harnett County, North Carolina was given the name *Barbecue Swamp* by a settler named Red Neill McNeill. It is believed that the mist rising from the swamp reminded him of the slow smoking barbecue fires he had seen while exploring the West Indies.

Totally Q

1757: Barbecue Presbyterian Church was founded by Scottish settlers in Harnett County, North Carolina.

1766: Royal Governor William Tryon held a barbecue in Wilmington, North Carolina as a gesture of good will. Members of a local patriot group known as the Sons of Liberty were a bit peeved at the Crown's recent passage of the Stamp Act, so to show their displeasure, they arrived at the party unannounced, dumped out the beer and tossed the freshly barbecued oxen into the river. Of course we rarely hear about this act, deferring instead to the more-heralded "Boston Tea Party" which was still seven years in the future.

1769: An entry in George Washington's diary read: "Went up to Alexandria to a barbicue. Back in three nights."

1773: Another entry in Washington's diary noted that he attended a "Barbicue of my own giving at Accatinck [sic]."

1793: After using his masonry skills to lay the cornerstone for the Capitol building in Washington, D.C., George Washington threw a barbecue celebration that featured a roasted 500-pound ox.

1805: Notes from the diary of Joseph Whitehouse indicate that the Lewis and Clark expedition carried and used Dutch Ovens.

1816: Noah Webster, who hailed from Connecticut, included a notation in his *Collection of Words and Phrases* that barbecue was, "used in the Southern states."

1822: Charles Lamb (1775-1834) first published *A Dissertation Upon Roast Pig*.

1829: Supporters of presidential candidate Andrew Jackson were labeled by the *National Intelligence*, a newspaper of the day, as "barbacues[sic] ."

1830: Skilton Dennis of Ayden, North Carolina began to roast whole hogs for large church camp meetings that were held in the area. According to historians, Dennis used to load his chuck wagon with barbecued meats and take his offerings on the road.

1834: One of the first barbecues featuring mutton was held to celebrate the Fourth of July on the banks of the Ohio River in Owensboro, Kentucky.

1853: Stafford, Texas used barbecue to celebrate their town's addition as a new stop on the BBB&C Railroad.

Totally Q

1860: The American Party sponsored the Great American Barbecue in Austin, Texas. They invited all the citizens of Texas to attend, and admittance was free. The featured speaker was Sam Houston.

1865: The Chicago Stockyards opened, consolidating many of the smaller operations scattered around the city.

1869: A large barbecue in Kansas City was held to celebrate the opening of the Hannibal Bridge over the Missouri River.

1867: A German butcher named Charles Feltman (1841-1910) opened the very first Coney Island hot dog stand in Brooklyn, NY.

1871: Forward-thinking entrepreneurs developed and placed into service the nation's first refrigerated railcars. These cars were used to haul cattle, and were instrumental in the development of the modern-day beef industry.

1876: At the Great Centennial Exposition in Philadelphia, the H. J. Heinz pickle company first introduced their version of bottled catsup. Since that time, the recipe has remained relatively unchanged.

1882: The first-ever refrigeration system was installed on a steamship. The compartment was used to transport beef from Argentina to Europe and resulted in what would become known as a "beef boom."

1885: Some say the first hamburger was served by its inventor Charles Nagreen at the Outagamie County Fair in Seymour, Wisconsin.

1891: Townsfolk from Whitney, Texas were concerned about losing population and decided to hold a barbecue to promote residency. More than a ton and a half of barbecued meats were prepared and given away in the effort.

1893: The Columbian Exposition caused thousands of hungry fairgoers to descend on the city of Chicago. It is believed by some hot dog historians (yes, this is an actual area of expertise) that the hot dog (then called a dachshund sausage) was first served by vendors there. It was a hit. Additionally, in 1893, "little dogs" were first served at a baseball game, allegedly in St. Louis at the Browns home baseball stadium, beginning a long-term love affair that continues today.

1895: Louis Lassen began to operate a lunch wagon on Meadow Street in New Haven, Connecticut, serving steak and ground steak sandwiches. The original sandwiches were made from trimmings and scraps and are considered by some to be the forerunner of the hamburger. In 1907, the business moved into a permanent structure, and even though Louis' Lunch restaurant has changed location several times, it is still in operation today, run by the fourth generation of the Lassen family.

Totally Q

1896: Pennsylvanian Joseph Lodge constructed a cast iron foundry in South Pittsburg, Tennessee and began to manufacture cast iron cookware under the name of Lodge. One of their most popular items at the time was the Dutch Oven. The foundry has expanded and is still in operation.

1897: Ellsworth B. A. Zwoyer patented a design for charcoal briquettes.

1904: Hungry fans arriving at a Yale-Harvard football game by railcar began to bring along picnic baskets to enjoy at the field, which is believed to be the origin of modern "tailgating."

1907: Henry Perry, who is considered by some to be the "Father of Kansas City Barbecue," opened what is arguably the first indoor sit-down barbecue restaurant in Kansas City. After Henry passed, the business was sold to Charlie Bryant, one of his workers. When Charlie passed, his brother Arthur took over and founded the iconic and still-thriving Arthur Bryant's Barbecue restaurants.

1912: A large barbecue was held for railroad workers to celebrate the line reaching O'Donnell, Texas.

1913: Aluminum foil was first used to wrap candy bars, Life Savers, and gum. Later uses would include all forms of outdoor cooking.

1913: Martha McCullogh-Williams wrote *Dishes and Beverages of the Old South*, which included descriptions of cooking techniques that used green wood spits, trenches, coal, and mop sauces to slow cook various kinds of freshly killed meats.

1916: Nathan Handwerker (1892-1974), an employee of Charles Feldman, started Nathan's Famous by opening a stand on Coney Island near Surf and Stillwell Avenues. He sold hot dogs for five cents each.

1916: The first Nathan's Famous Fourth of July Hot Dog Eating Contest was held on Coney Island. James Mullen was the winner.

1917: The Carolina Beverage Company of Salisbury, North Carolina began to distribute Cheerwine, a cherry flavored soda. The drink is a favorite in the South, especially when eating barbecue.

1918: A barbecue restaurant opened in Owensboro, Kentucky specializing in barbecued mutton. The joint was named Old Hickory Bar-B-Q Pit and was run by Charles "Pappy" Forman. Members of his family operate the establishment under the same name today.

1920: Henry Ford built one of the first plants that converted scrap wood to charcoal briquettes.

Totally Q

1922: Leonard's Pit Barbecue of Memphis opened its doors.

1924: The Chicago Stockyards hit their peak during this year with more than 18.6 million cattle, hogs and sheep passing through the gates on their way to America's markets.

1925: Big Bob Gibson first began serving customers his barbecue in Decatur, Alabama.

1926: A Texan named Edgar Davis received a huge settlement when he sold his holdings in Luling Oil. To celebrate, he threw a huge barbecue, which was attended by an estimated 35,000 of his closest friends and family members.

1931: The Santa Maria Club of California hosted their first "Stag Barbecue."

1932: Black's Barbecue of Lockhart, Texas opened its doors and remains in business today, owned and operated by the same family.

1935: Porky Pig appeared in his first cartoon, *I Haven't Got a Hat*. Although his role in this feature was minor, Porky went on to become one of the most popular and influential members of the swine community.

1935: Previously available only in bottles, beer was first sold in a can. This was a great advancement in the science of beer drinking, which has direct ties to grilling and barbecue.

1936: President Roosevelt served hot dogs to the king and queen of England, despite protests from some of America's upper crust.

1938: The *Sunset Barbecue Cook Book* was first published. This book, considered by some to be one of the first definitive books written on the topic, has been periodically updated and remains in print today.

1940: Manufacturers of hot dogs began to package their product in packs of ten. Stubborn bakers, apparently upset at not being notified of the change, agreed in a secret meeting to begin offering rolls in packs of only eight.

1941: To celebrate his victory, newly elected Texas governor W. Lee "Pappy" O'Daniel had several large pits dug on the grounds of the Capitol building in Austin. He held a party and gave away free barbecue to anyone who showed up.

1942: Hot dogs dipped in cornmeal batter,

known as "corn dogs," were introduced at the Texas State Fair.

1946: Gates Bar-B-Q original restaurant opened in Kansas City at Nineteenth and Vine.

1946: Legend has it that Leonard's Pit Barbecue of Memphis, Tennessee started adding coleslaw to their pulled pork sandwiches. What a great idea!

1948: The Hasty-Bake Charcoal Oven was first introduced by Grant "Hasty" Hastings and is still in production today.

1948: H.J. Heinz introduced the first barbecue sauce for nationwide distribution.

1950s: Warner Raleigh of North Carolina first combined hushpuppies with barbecued foods.

1952: Bob Schultz, a meat cutter from Santa Maria, California, threaded a cut of meat he had been using for grinds onto a spit, added some seasonings and tossed it onto his grill. After an hour or so, he took it off and sliced it thinly against the grain. Bob and his butcher buddies liked it and some now say this was the origin of the popular tri-tip cut.

1952: A welder for Weber Brothers Metal Works named George Stephen made the prototype for the Weber Kettle...and the rest is history.

1952: The first chili cook-off was held at the Texas State Fair. These contests are considered the forerunners of today's barbecue cook-offs.

1959: What some refer to as the first-ever barbecue cook-off was held in the state of Hawaii. It was a "men only" event and was called the Kaiser Foil Cook-off.

1960: It was during the 60s that the first gas fueled grills were manufactured by the W.C. Bradley Company, which later distributed them under the name of Char-Broil.

1961: The W.C. Bradley Company (Char-Broil), filed for a patent for a grease handling system to be used on an outdoor grill.

1962: On July 24, Wilbur's Barbecue opened its doors in Goldsboro, North Carolina. Over the years, some of their customers have included Presidents George W. Bush Sr. and Bill Clinton, North Carolina Governors Hunt and Sanford, and U. S. Senator Jesse Helms.

Totally Q

1964: On November 12, President Lyndon Baines Johnson hosted his first state dinner to honor the President-elect of Mexico. The event was catered by Walter Jetton, Johnson's long-time pitmaster of choice. On the menu that evening was, of course, barbecue.

1964: Spicy hot chicken wings were first served at the Anchor Bar in Buffalo, New York. These wings later became known as Buffalo wings.

1967: Herbert Oyler of Mesquite, Texas applied for, and was given, a patent for one of the first barbecue units that used a rotisserie to move the meat around in the cooking chamber.

1968: McDonald's introduced the Big Mac, which sold for 49 cents.

1968: Floyd "Sonny" Tillman opened his first barbecue restaurant in Gainesville, Florida. The name was eventually changed to Sonny's Real Pit BBQ.

1971: What was billed as "the world's largest fly-in barbecue" was held at the Fort Frances Airport in Ontario, Canada July 1-10. A promotional blurb in *Flying* Magazine advised that attendees should, "Bring your own sauce."

1971: The Union Stock Yard and Transit Company (the Chicago Stockyards, for short) closed forever. Once known as the "Hog Butcher for the World," this operation employed more than 40,000 workers at its peak.

1972: North Carolina Governor Bob Scott declared his state to be "The Pig Pickin' Capital of the World."

1974: The first-ever barbecue contest was added to the long-running Houston Livestock Show and Rodeo.

1974: The *Adam's Rib's* episode of the hit television show *M*A*S*H* first aired.

1974: Ole Hickory Pits, a division of David B. Knight and Associates Inc., based in Cape Girardeau, Missouri, was first founded.

1974: Ed Fisher opened the first Big Green Egg Store in Atlanta, Georgia, offering one of the first commercially manufactured ceramic cooker/smokers to the public.

1976: Mike Robertson and B.B. Robertson from Decatur, Illinois began to distribute their own brand of rotating barbecue cooker under the name of Southern Pride.

1976: The first *wagyu* cattle were imported into the United States from Japan. *Wagyu* means "Japanese cow."

1977: Sonny" Tillman began to franchise his small group of Florida barbecue restaurants, which eventually grew into one of the largest national barbecue chains.

1977: The W.C. Bradley Company launched its subsidiary known as Char-Broil and was the first to package an LP tank and gas grill in one box. They also became a leading manufacturer of electric grills, portable gas grills and table-top portable grills.

1978: A shopper named Ella Whitt purchased the first pound of meat carrying the name "Certified Angus Beef" at Renzett's IGA in Columbus, Ohio.

1978: The first Memphis in May World Championship Barbecue Cooking Contest was held in Memphis, Tennessee with 26 competing teams. Today there are more than 250 teams cooking in the event with crowd numbers routinely exceeding an estimated 100,000.

1980: Meadow Creek began distributing its line of smokers and grills from a shop located in Lancaster County, Pennsylvania.

1980: The first American Royal Barbecue Contest was held in Kansas City, Missouri.

1981: Weber first introduced the popular Smokey Mountain Cooker.

1981: The McRib sandwich was introduced in some McDonald's restaurants around the country. There is some dispute as to whether this product bears any resemblance to actual barbecue (or real meat, for that matter).

1981: John Marshall wrote a master's thesis titled *Barbecue in Western Kentucky: An Ethnographic Study*.

1982: The first Big Pig Jig was held in Vienna, Georgia with 20 teams that cooked whole hog only. The winner that year was Stump & Son from Marietta, Georgia. This event now draws over 120 teams and hosts more than 10,000 spectators each year.

1982: The first annual Mike Royko Ribfest was held in Chicago's Grant Park, located on the shores of Lake Michigan. Royko was a columnist for the *Chicago Sun-Times*. The event attracted more than 400 teams and was won by Charlie Robinson, who went on to open a restaurant and develop his own line of sauces and rubs.

1983: Paul Kirk, championship pitmaster, cookbook author, professional chef, Order of the Magic Mop , and barbecue instructor was given the title "The Baron of Barbecue" by Kansas City radio personality Mike Murphy.

1983: Pitt's and Spitt's pitbuilders opened its first retail store in Houston, Texas.

1984: The International Dutch Oven Society was formed.

1984: The Ph.B., or Doctor of Barbecue Philosophy degree, was first conceived by Ardie Davis (a.k.a. Remus Powers) from Kansas City. The same year, he penned the

Totally Q

oath for the Diddy-Wa-Diddy National Barbecue Sauce Contest which was adopted by KCBS several years later and is still in use today.

1985: Mike Mills bought a local bar and grill in Murphysboro, Illinois and named it the 17th Street Bar & Grill.

1985: Chef Larry from Chicago, Illinois entered his family's barbecue sauce in the Mike Royko Rib Cookoff. He finished a respectable second in a field of more than 700 entries, but it wasn't long before the sauce was on its way to becoming one of the top-selling barbecue sauces in the country. Today, the Sweet Baby Ray brand, named for Chef Larry's brother, David, who picked up the nickname on the basketball courts of Chicago's west side, sells more than 500,000 cases a year.

KANSAS CITY BARBEQUE ★ SOCIETY ★

1985: March 5 is a day that will live forever in the annals of pig history. A hog by the name of "Bud" was sold for the staggering sum of $56,000.

1986: A sausage measuring 5,917 feet was cooked in Barcelona, Spain. I wonder how big the bun was.

1986: BBQ Pits by Klose was founded by David Klose of Houston, Texas.

1986: The Kansas City Barbeque Society (KCBS) was formed.

1986: Rich Davis, the creator of KC Masterpiece Barbecue Sauce, sold the brand to the Kingsford Division of the Clorox Company (the makers of Kingsford Charcoal).

1987: Kraft Foods began nationwide distribution of Bulls-Eye brand barbecue sauce.

1987: Mike McGowan of Dixie, Louisiana began to manufacture and distribute Backwoods Smokers.

1987: The city of Frankfurt, Germany celebrated the 500th birthday of the hot dog.

1988: Lang BBQ Smokers was founded in Nahunta, Georgia.

1989: The Traeger Company began nationwide distribution of their growing line of pellet-fueled barbecue grills.

1989: The first Jack Daniel's World Championship Invitational Barbecue contest was held at the Jack Daniel's distillery in Lynchburg, Tennessee.

1989: The judge's oath written by Ardie Davis (a.k.a. Remus Powers, Ph.B.) was first used to swear in judges at KCBS-sanctioned contests.

Totally Q

1990: The Memphis in May World Championship Barbecue Cooking Contest was recognized in the 1990 edition of the *Guinness Book of World Records* as the "largest barbecue."

1990: BBQ TV had its beginning on the World Wide Web.

1990: The first edition of *The National Barbecue News* was published in Douglas, Georgia.

1991: The first meeting of the Pacific Northwest Barbecue Association was held.

1991: The XIT Ranch held its annual reunion in Dalhart, Texas. It is a known fact that everything is bigger in Texas, and this affair was no different. Pits were dug using backhoes in order to cook 11,000 pounds of beef, which was then served to more than 20,000 guests.

1991: The National Barbecue Association (NBBQA), was first formed as a nonprofit trade association to address the needs of the broad, diverse and growing barbecue industry. They incorporated in the state of North Carolina in 1993.

1991: The New England Barbecue Society was first formed as the New England Society for Wood Cookery. The name was changed in 1994.

1992: Christopher B. "Stubb" Stubblefield of Austin, Texas began to manufacture and distribute his line of barbecue sauces under the name of Stubb's. The first two flavors were Original and Spicy. The line later included additional flavors, marinades and a variety of spice rubs.

1993: Cooper's Old Time Pit Bar-B-Que opened in Llano, Texas.

1993: The Food Network started regular broadcasting on cable TV. Today this programming is seen in more than 100 million households across America and over 150 countries around the world.

1994: The Texas Gulf Coast BBQ Cookers Association was chartered.

1994: "Famous Dave" Anderson opened his first restaurant under the name of "Famous Dave's BBQ Shack," in Haywood, Minnesota.

1994: Ed "Fast Eddy" Maurin began to manufacture Fast Eddy Cookers, one of the first wood pellet-fueled BBQ smokers.

1995: The first Ribfest was held by the Burlington Lakeshore Rotary Club in Burlington, Ontario Canada. In 2009, the festival rebranded itself as "Canada's Largest Ribfest." The attendance that year was estimated at more than 175,000 and 150,000 pounds of ribs were consumed, prepared by eighteen "Ribber Teams" from across North America.

Totally Q

1995: The BBQ Forum was first posted on the Internet by Ray Basso.

1995: Grillin' N' Chillin' (starring Bobby Flay and Jack McDavid) made its network debut on the Food Network.

1996: The Lone Star Barbecue Society was founded in Texas.

1996: Oklahoma Joe's opened its first barbecue joint in Stillwater, Oklahoma. This location was later closed and today is headquartered in Kansas City, Kansas.

1996: The Minnesota Barbecue Society was formed.

1996: Myron Mixon of Jack's Old South Barbecue entered his first competition, the Lock & Dam BBQ Contest, held in Augusta, Georgia. He took first place in whole hog and ribs, along with a third place in shoulder. Pretty impressive for a first outing, wouldn't you say?

1996: Lynx Professional Grills was founded.

1997: The Char-Broil company acquired the New Braunfels Smoker Company of New Braunfels, Texas, which had been a leader in the manufacture of heavy duty charcoal grills, smokers and other accessories. This same year Char-Broil also purchased the barbecue grill division of the Thermos Company of Schaumburg, Illinois.

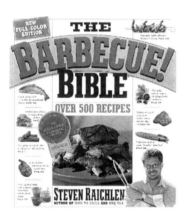

1998: One equipment trade group estimated that 11.6 million grills were shipped to retailers during this year. That same group stated that more than 2.9 *billion* barbecue events were held throughout the world.

1998: Workman Publishing Company released Steven Raichlen's The Barbecue Bible. This book has since sold more than 900,000 copies and has received numerous awards and accolades.

2000: The first meeting of the Florida Bar-B-Que Association was held.

2000: Ray Lampe (a.k.a. Dr. BBQ) left his family business and longtime trucking career and moved from Chicago to Florida to begin working as an outdoor cooking guru. Today, Ray is the author of numerous cookbooks and is seen regularly on various network and cable television channels.

2000: Chris Lilly of Big Bob Gibson's Barbecue won his first Grand Championship at the Memphis in May Barbecue Contest. His team won top honors again in 2003 and 2011.

Totally Q

2001: The Orrison family opened their first barbecue and blues joint called The Shed in Ocean Springs, Mississippi. Today their mantra, "get fed at the shed" is well known throughout the entire barbecue world. The chain now includes five additional locations from Louisiana to Florida.

2001: According to the Weber *Grillwatch Survey*, more than 4,000,000 portable grills were purchased for tailgating events.

2001: Myron Mixon (a.k.a. "The Winningest Man in Barbecue") of Jack's Old South Barbecue, won the first of his three World Championships at the Memphis in May barbecue contest. He captured the same title in 2004 and 2007. Additionally, Myron and his team took first place in whole hog at this event in 2001, 2003, 2004 and 2007.

2003: Phil Rizzardi started the *BBQ Brethren Forum* at www.bbq-bretheren.com. The site remains very popular.

2004: The Pennsylvania Barbecue Association was formed. It was renamed the Mid-Atlantic Barbecue Association in 2005.

2004: The California Barbecue Association was formed.

2004: ESPN began live coverage of the Nathan's Fourth of July Hot Dog Eating Contest on Coney Island. The network reported that 926,000 people tuned in to watch that year, and by 2011 the audience increased to 1.9 million.

2004: The South Carolina Barbecue Association was first organized by Lake E. High Jr. and Walter G. Rolandi, Ph.D.

2004: The BBQ Guru temperature control device was first introduced on the market.

2004: Walter "Stump" McDowell quit his full time job in the heating and air conditioning business and began to manufacture and distribute his line of gravity-fed charcoal smokers under the name Stump's Smokers. The company's mantra is "Stump don't build no junk."

2005: The website *Amazingribs.com* made its debut. The site was created by Craig "Meathead" Goldwyn and today is one of the most heavily-traveled barbecue sites on the Internet.

2006: The Georgia Barbecue Association was formed in Fort Valley, GA.

2006: According to the ATA, (American Tailgaters Association) and the November issue of *Sports Insight* magazine, somewhere between 20-50 million Americans par-

Totally Q

ticipated in tailgating activities for the year. If you ask me, 30 million plus or minus is a pretty wide range.

2006: Char-Broil introduced the first line of infrared gas grills.

2006: Green Mountain Grills LLC of Reno, Nevada was established.

2007: New York's Institute of Culinary Education sponsored a four day field trip called Camp BBQ, which took students to various barbecue joints throughout North Carolina. Eating barbecue for a grade? Sign me up!

2007: The Great Lakes Barbecue Association was formed.

2007: Char-Broil released the "Big Easy," an oil-less infrared turkey fryer.

2008: In Paraguay enthusiastic cooks grilled nearly 61,000 pounds of beef on a mile-long grill using six tons of charcoal. The event was known locally as "*Todo bicho que camina va al asador,*" which loosely translates to "Every critter walking goes to the barbecue."

2008: The much-anticipated 22 ½-inch Smokey Mountain smoker was introduced by Weber.

2009: The first episode of *BBQ Pitmasters* was broadcast December 3 on the TLC Network. Produced by John Markus, the show's cameras followed several cook teams as they competed in various barbecue competitions across the country.

2009: Joey Chestnut set the world record for the Nathan's Hot Dog Eating Contest, held July Fourth on Coney Island, New York, by eating 68 hot dogs in 10 minutes.

2009: Harry Soo and his competition barbecue team named Slap Yo' Daddy BBQ took first place in all four categories in the KCBS-sanctioned Way Out West BBQ Championship in Stockton, California. This was one of the first teams ever to sweep the championship.

2009: Aaron and Stacey Franklin opened Franklin's Barbecue in East Austin, Texas. They completely sold out of brisket that first day and amazingly, have continued to do so each and every day up to the present. In 2010, they were named "The Best Barbecue Restaurant in America" by *Bon Appetit* Magazine.

2009: Carson Rotisseries was established in Memphis, Tennessee by Blake Carson.

2010: Jimmy Dean died at age 81. This country music singer, founded Jimmy Dean

28

Meats in 1969 and became widely known for his Jimmy Dean brand sausage.

2011: The current world record hot dog, which measured almost 670 feet long, was made in Asuncion, Paraguay. The bun alone weighed 330 pounds. After the giant wiener was certified by authorities from the *Guinness Book of World Records*, it was sliced up and eaten by the large crowd that was on hand.

2011: For the first time in its 94-year history, the Nathan's Hot Dog Eating Contest held separate events for men and women. *You've come a long way, baby.*

2012: Season 3 of *BBQ Pitmasters* was broadcast on the Destination America Channel.

2012: The Food Network show *Chopped* aired a five-part series featuring a grilling tournament in Tucson, Arizona where the top prize was $50,000. The series was called *Grill Masters*.

2013: The best-selling compendium of barbecue wisdom by George Hensler titled *Totally Q* was published. And that, my friends, concludes our history.

Burnt Ends

"No matter how much you get involved in barbecue as a lifestyle, summer is still the king when it comes to grilling, slow smoking, and the parties we call barbecues." —Ray "Dr. BBQ" Lampe

"If a culture develops barbecue too early, lesser inventions like writing and the wheel go ignored." —*The Man's Book of BBQ* by Brendan McGinley

"If Fred Flintstone knew that large order of ribs would tip his car over, why did he order them at the end of every show?" —Steven Wright

"We're not against progress; we're just preserving the original traditions that eventually launched the naked ape to the moon. It's imperative in all human discovery and adventure to find new and interesting things, and spit roast them." —*The Man's Book of BBQ* by Brendan McGinley

"In the South, especially, but everywhere else too, save the deepest sheep or cattle country, the fortune of barbecue has always been tied to the fortune of the pig." —John Thorne

Totally Q

"You cannot learn barbecue, you live barbecue."
—Michael Conrad, Barbecue Center, Lexington, North Carolina

"The story of barbecue is the story of America: Settlers arrive on great unspoiled continent, discover wondrous riches, set them on fire and eat them." —Vince Staten

"You can't perfume a hog." —Lewis Grizzard

Fire, meat and smoke...livin' the barbecue dream.
Photo by Rick Browne, courtesy of Sunbelt Archives.

 # It's A Caveman Thang: BBQ History

I t's hard to be exact when speaking about the origins of barbecue and grilling, especially when describing the early days of 'cue. It would be much easier to determine the origins of modern-day 'cueology if we used the time frame beginning from when Man (and I am using the term *Man* here to include mankind, both male and female) began to treat outdoor cookery as a "fun" or "leisure time" activity. The other reason I would prefer not to reach back too far on the topic is that folks might not like what I find, particularly when talking about significant firsts such as *Who was the Father (or Mother) of barbecue?*

Seems to me that if someone really decided to burn some brain cells on the topic, they might determine, in fact, that WOMEN were the first barbecuers. Think about it: In the very early days, men were the hunter-gatherers and women raised the young 'uns, kept the domicile and almost undoubtedly cooked the food.

I realize that the majority of modern-day male outdoor cooks would prefer not to think that their revered pastime was started by some cavewoman carrying a baby on her back while flipping a dinosaur roast over the fire pit, but boys, that's probably the way it went down. Most of us males who consider ourselves—at least in our own minds—to be pitmasters, prefer to believe that the origins of modern outside cooking were in the early 1950s. This was a time when a smartly dressed man—wearing a barbecue apron, occasionally a chef's hat, and sometimes smoking a pipe—stood guard over the backyard barbecue pit on many a summer's evening. Chances are, he would be sipping a glass of bourbon and chatting with some similarly dressed male companions (minus the aprons and hats). In most of these nostalgic memory fabrications, the women would be in the background, sitting around chatting or possibly setting the table. Yes, the backyard cooking arena was the man's domain—at least that's what we men would like to believe.

Fast forward to today: While the outdoor cooking scene is somewhat dominated by the male gender, there are many up-and-coming and established female pitmasters

Totally Q

out there and in the world of competition barbecue, the number of female cooks is growing, as well. Many of the more established women of the smoke routinely trounce the field of entrants, completely disregarding the fact that most of the team leaders are males (and supposedly more dominant when it comes to cooking out-of-doors).

In the interest of inclusion and diversity, I would like to be the first male to say thanks to all of those cavewomen who got us headed in the right direction when it came to cooking in the great outdoors. Now, as we continue through history, I invite you to pull up a chair, sit back and relax—you're about to embark on a fun-filled, action-packed journey down barbecue lanel hope you enjoy the ride.

Taking Our 'Cues from the Past
Residents of central Europe really knew how to throw a barbecue! According to the September/October 2009 issue of *Archaeology Magazine*, excavations at a 31,000-year-old site in the Czech Republic uncovered a cooking pit with the remains

of two mammoths in addition to some other smaller animals. What is not known for sure is what type of sauce was used.

It's a Caveman Thang
World Champion Pitmaster Jim "Arkansas Trav'ler" Quessenberry explained the fascination many men have with barbecue: "It's the caveman in us. I think that's why you see more and more men barbecuing. It's a macho thing. Playing with fire and being outdoors, bragging about how good you cook, it's got all the macho rush to it without any of the violence. Also women do not pursue it very thoroughly. That's one territory they don't try to invade. They kind of leave it to us."

Totally Q

Cro-Vegan Man?

Go back thousands of years and consider this scenario: Hotshot village hunter Og has just slain a beast and hauled it back to camp. After receiving the expected accolades, the beast is butchered and then promptly roasted (no refrigeration, remember). Amidst all this excitement, I can't imagine anyone then suggesting to the camp cook that he toss some seaweed or *foozia* onto the grill because someone in the tribe is a vegan! It's my belief that any such prehistoric herbivore would probably have found himself searching for another tribal fire or covert veggie roast to warm his tookus by.

Yes Virginia, There *is* a Patron Saint of BBQ

Saint Alexander of Comana was known as "the charcoal burner." History tells us he was given this distinction because, acting strictly out of humility, he had taken up the job of burning charcoal. As a result of his chosen profession, he is also renowned for being filthy dirty most of the time. In an ultimate twist of fate, historians also tell us that Saint Alexander was burned to death in the year 251 during the persecution of Emperor Decius.

Saint Alexander of Comana, patron saint of BBQ.

Even Homer Liked 'Cue, and I'm Not Talking About Simpson

Back around 1260, Homer of *The Iliad* fame was thought to have said, "Many a goodly ox, with many a sheep and bleating goat did they butcher and cut up; many a tusked bore moreover, fat and well fed, did they singe and set to roast in the flames of Vulcan." I have just two questions: *Did they have Vulcan appliances back then, and when is the last time you or one of your friends used the word "moreover"?*

Rotisserie History

Rotisserie history: try saying that five times fast, especially after two or three beers. The idea of turning meats over a fire certainly isn't a new one; the French word first appeared in Paris shops around 1450. Of course, it goes without saying that something we almost take for granted today wasn't always as convenient or easy to use.

Totally Q

Back in the earliest rotisserie days, meat was turned by a young male servant, who was referred to as a "spit boy" or "spit jack." The first mechanized turnspits were canine-powered, followed by clockwork and steam powered units. Some clever and lazy pitmaster even devised a spit that had a set of gears powered by a turbine; the device was mounted in the chimney and turned by the rising heat. Perhaps this could be noted as one of the earliest forms of "green" power.

Another environmentally responsible power source came from a unique breed of dog that you won't ever see on reruns of the *Westminster Dog Show* because it is now extinct. These short-legged, long-bodied dogs, with faces only a mother could love, were bred to run on a wheel that turned a rotisserie in order to slow-cook meat over a fire. This breed was known as the Kitchen Dog, the Cooking Dog, the Turnspit Dog, the Vernepator, or, for those who read Latin, *Canis vertigus*. It was also mentioned in the 1576 book *Of English Dogs* under the name *Turnespete*. Known for their extreme loyalty, these dogs had to be courageous while working in areas of extreme heat and obedient enough not to "woof down" the subject of their efforts.

Today, we're lucky to have electric-powered rotisseries which make life much more relaxed and enjoyable for everyone involved. Because of this technology, we can avoid all potential conflicts with child labor laws, as well as the wrath of PETA, who would protest not only our meat-eating habits, but the practice of using dogs to power our cookers!

A turnspit dog hard at work (you can see it up in the wheel near the ceiling).

Totally Q

Once Upon a Time in America...

Journalist and food writer Betty Wason (1912-2001) had this to say about the early evolution of American barbecue: "When the European invaders brought livestock to Mexico—pigs and sheep and cattle—the meat of these animals was cut up to be roasted over the barbecue frames, and the barbecue in the Caribbean became an outdoor feast equivalent to the clambake in New England. The custom would travel north, into Colonial Georgia and Maryland and Pennsylvania, and the Spanish colonizers would take it as far west as California, where in time the spicy-hot sauces or *moles* of Mexican cooks served over roasted beef or pork would become eternally known as *barbecue sauces.*"

Just Give Us a Time Machine and We'll Be There

In her *West Coast Cook Book*, Helen Evans Brown described early barbecue in the Land of Fruits and Nuts: "Way back when the Dons first came to California, grilled meat was a part of every festive gathering. A huge fire was made, a freshly killed beef hung in the shade of a tree, and *vaqueros* and their ladies cut off pieces every time that hunger called, and cooked it over the waiting fire. It wasn't only charcoal grilling that was practiced by those Californians of the past, they also had their huge pit barbecues even as today."

Going Whole Hog

An early cookbook by R. Bradley, written in 1732 and called *The Country Housewife and the Lady's Director in the Management of a House, and the Delights and Profits of a Farm*, talked about preparing a whole hog for the pit. In my opinion, it is also an early mention of barbecue sauce. What follows is the original transcript from the book as reported by Steven Raichlen in his bestselling book, *BBQ USA*:

Take a hog of five or six months old, kill it, and take out its innards....then stretch out the ribs, and open the belly, as wide as may be: then strew into it what pepper and salt you please.

After this, take a large gridiron, and set it upon a stand of iron, about three foot and a half high, and upon that, lay your hog open'd as above, with the belly side downwards, and with a good clear fire of charcoal under. Broil [grill] that side till it is enough, flouring the back at the same time often. Memorandum, this should be done in a yard, or garden, with a covering like a tent over it.

When the belly part of the hog is enough, and turn'd upwards, and well fix'd, to be steady upon the grid-iron, or barbecue, pour into the belly of the hog, three or four quarts of water, and half as much white wine, and as much salt as you will, with some sage cut small; adding the peels of six or eight lemons, and an ounce of fresh clove.

Totally Q

Then let it broil [grill] till it is enough, which will be, from beginning to end, about eight hours; and when you serve it, pour the sauce, and lay it in a dish, with the back upwards. Memorandum, the skin must not be cut before you lay it on the gridiron, to keep in the gravey.

Oh, Those Tarheel Piglovers
William Byrd, in his eighteenth-century book *The Secret History of the Dividing Line Betwixt Virginia and North Carolina,* had some pretty snippy things to say about some Southerners' predilection for pork. He wrote that hog meat was: "The staple commodity of North Carolina . . . and with pitch and tar makes up the whole of their traffic . . . these people live so much upon swine's flesh that it don't only incline them to the yaws*, and consequently to the . . . [loss] of their noses, but makes them likewise extremely hoggish in their temper, and many of them seem to grunt rather than speak in their ordinary conversation."

*Yaws is an infectious tropical disease closely related to syphilis. Perhaps this is why Virginia is frequently considered beyond the parameters of the "barbecue belt." You sure don't want to have any yaws below the belt.

Mop Up
One of the first mentions of mops or basting sauces was found in a letter written by a Mr. Butler in Virginia to a friend in the year 1784, and more recently reported by Steve Raichlen in his book, *BBQ USA:* "Then they lay the meat over a wooden grate about six inches above the coals and then they keep basting it with a mixture of butter, salt and water, turning it every now and then until it is done." Some unofficial sources believe that this letter was an early form of what would become today's BBQ forums and chat rooms. These venues are wildly popular on the Internet today as places where followers of the sweet blue smoke post various methods and procedures associated with barbecue.

And You Know Where to Stick Those Lower Ranks, You Limey!
The Englishman Jonathan Weld, on his visit to the United States in 1799, showed his colors as an early barbecue snob: "The people are extremely fond of an entertainment which they call a barbecue. It consists of a large party of people meeting together to partake of a sturgeon or pig roasted while in the open air, on a sort of low hurdle, over a slow fire; this, however, is an entertainment confined chiefly to the lower ranks."

Porky Jones Was an Engineer...
As the population in many East Coast cities continued to increase in the 1800s, there

Totally Q

was a rising demand for fresh pork and other swine-related delicacies and some reports say that in the year 1826, more than 200,000 hogs were moved from the Kentucky/Tennessee area into North Carolina. Men tasked with driving these large herds of swine to market were called "drovers," and large trails were cleared in order to move the animals. One can imagine that a gang of 100 or so pigs moving together in one direction is going to clear a pretty wide swath all on its own, and it's my understanding that a number of these pathways eventually became some of the first railway routes.

A cowboy tending a Longhorn herd near Deanville Texas on a spur of the Chisolm trail, circa 1866.

Where's A Longhorn-Sized Coleman Cooler When You Need One?

After the Civil War (1861-1865) there were reported to be more than 3 million long-horn steers roaming the prairies of the West, and many of the former soldiers who moved to that region in search of opportunity eventually found work as cowhands. Their job was to round up this great herd of beef and get it to market.

Because refrigeration as we know it had yet to be invented and there was a shortage of both bagged ice and coolers around the country after the war, the chuck wagon cooks on these expeditions were often reluctant to waste a full-grown steer just to feed a small crew of cowpokes. Thanks to some Spanish settlers that moved into the area in the late 1600s, however, the plains were home to a burgeoning goat popula-tion and the cooks found that a 15- to 20-pound goat served quite well in feeding the men. During the three-month trail rides, they devised a variety of ways to prepare this

37

ubiquitous meat, which included: roasted goat, goat fricassee, goat stew, goat a-la-king, goat casserole, fried goat, goat meatballs, goat balls for meat, etc. Seems that just about any way Bubba Gump could cook shrimp, those trail cooks could prepare goat.

Avoiding BBQ Sauce Burns

One of the most popular early Southern cookbooks was *Mrs. Hill's New Cook Book*, which was published in 1867. In it, Annabella P. Hill shared her recipe for *Sauce for Barbecues*, a concoction that food historian Damon Fowler noted "was the Georgia classic until well into this century, and it is still favored in some parts of the state. Its advantage over modern sweet tomato sauce is that it is less likely to burn." Is this why Georgia and South Carolina barbecue sauces have mustard in them today?

The Official Birthplace of the Hamburger

The Library of Congress has certified that Louis' Lunch of New Haven, Connecticut was the American birthplace of the hamburger. Louis Lassen is recognized as the first person to put ground steak between two slices of bread back in the 1800s and this sandwich is made the very same way today by the fourth generation of the Lassen family. The burger, a blend of five meat cuts, is hand-formed into patties, which are then flamed broiled vertically in wire baskets and served between two slices of toasted white bread. The only available garnishes are cheese, tomato or onion. Ketchup, relish, mayonnaise and mustard are not available, so don't ask.

Early Incarnations of Barbecue Sauce

Early forms of the blends that one day would become known as barbecue sauce, began to appear in the early 1820s. The recipe was not tomato-based as we know it today, but included mushrooms, nuts, jellies and chutneys. Tomato sauces and ketchups had yet to find their way onto grocers' shelves or into the home pantry, as the tomato was still considered poisonous.

Now THAT'S a Party!

In 1880, Alexander Sweet and John Knox described the enormity of their first barbecue experience: "We arrived on the barbecue grounds at about ten o'clock. More than two thousand people had already arrived, some from a distance of forty to fifty miles...A deep trench, three hundred feet long, had been dug. This trench was filled from end to end with glowing coals; and suspended over them on horizontal poles were the carcasses of forty animals–sheep, hogs, oxen, and deer–roasting over the slow fire...It is claimed that this primitive method of preparation is the perfection of cookery, and that no meat tastes so sweet as that which is barbecued."

Totally Q

This Guy Had a Serious Thing About Fat

Here we read about the joys of roasting a whole hog as described in the 1904 essay by Charles Lamb titled *A Dissertation Upon Roasted Pig*:

"He must be roasted. I am not ignorant that our ancestors ate them seethed, or boiled—but what a sacrifice of the exterior tegument! There is no flavour comparable, I will contend, to that of the crisp, tawny, well-watched, not over-roasted, crackling, as it is well called—the very teeth are invited to their share of the pleasure at this banquet in overcoming the coy, brittle resistance—with the adhesive oleaginous—O call it not fat—but an indefinable sweetness growing up to it—the tender blossoming of fat—fat cropped in the bud—taken in the shoot—in the first innocence—the cream and quintessence of the child-pig's yet pure food—the lean, no lean, but a kind of animal manna—or, rather, fat and lean (if it must be so) so blended and running into each other, that both together make but one ambrosian result, or common substance[sic]."

Henry T. Ford was about a lot more than the Model T.

Henry T. Ford, King of Charcoal

Henry Ford was looking for something useful to do with the scrap wood generated from the process of building Model T automobiles. After having a few drinks with his friend Thomas Edison, he came up with an idea and in 1920, built a plant to convert the scraps of wood to charcoal. Some time later, during a cookout at Henry's house, a relative named E.G. Kingsford mentioned that he knew of a site that could be used to construct a new and improved plant. The site was purchased, and eventually the

39

Totally Q

company's name was changed from Ford Charcoal to Kingsford Charcoal in E.G's honor. Today the Kingsford brand in its familiar red, white, and blue bag remains the largest producer of charcoal—and according to the Kingsford website, the facility converts more than one million tons of scrap wood each year into their famous briquettes.

Buy a Car, Get a Grill!
Always the innovator, Henry Ford often was involved in winning marketing ploys. In his spare time, he came up with the design for a small, portable grilling unit that could be fueled with his newly manufactured charcoal briquettes. He used the grill as an enticement for folks interested in buying one of his Model A or Model T Fords: *Buy a car, get a grill*—not a bad deal. This was back when you didn't have to take out a second mortgage to buy a new vehicle, which, of course, was a long time ago, in a galaxy far, far away...

The Father of Briquettes?
A resident of Pennsylvania, Ellsworth B. A. Zwoyer patented a design for charcoal briquettes in 1897. He was the founder of the Zwoyer Fuel Company which built charcoal briquette manufacturing plants in Buffalo, New York and Fall River, Massachusetts.

And Some Were Probably from Hamburg
According to food and travel writer Sharon Hudgins, "Around the turn of the century, German and Czech butchers in small towns in central Texas devised a profitable way to use up their unsold and less desirable cuts of meat. In addition to making sausages out of the meat scraps, they built enclosed barbecue pits in the back of their meat markets, and began smoke-roasting the meats they could not otherwise sell (tougher cuts, such as brisket and shoulder clods). Customers at the market could not only purchase fresh cuts of meat at the front counter, they could also eat hot-smoked meats in the back room of their shop. The combination of meat-market-and-barbecue-pit became a central Texas institution. Even today, many of the oldest and best Texas barbecue restaurants are run by families with German and Czech surnames."

Saved by the Steer
Here's a testimonial about the life-saving qualities of beef from Jane Trahey's 1949 *A Taste of Texas Cookbook:* "Beef cattle is still a basic industry in Texas, and beef a basic food. J. Frank Dobie, who has forgotten more about cattle than most people know the role that meat plays in a Texan's diet: An old rancher ate his usually hearty breakfast, which included several large chunks of beef, and then went out and promptly got himself shot in the stomach. The doctor who patched him up declared

it a phenomenon—that if it hadn't been for the beef, the bullet would have killed him."

Hot Wings
Back in the 50s and 60s, chicken wings were left on chicken pieces or used as fillers in a chicken box. That all changed in 1964. That's when the Bellisimo family, owners of the Anchor Bar in Buffalo, New York, decided to deep fry a few dozen wings, toss them in a spicy hot sauce, and serve them to customers. Little did they realize that this quick snack would eventually become a worldwide phenomenon, especially on a particular Sunday evening in February when a really big football game is played and a lot of "parties" are held. Today, the concept of "Buffalo" chicken now includes recipes for chicken wings, chicken fingers, popcorn chicken and even pizza, subs and salads.

Sex, Ribs, and Saltpeter
Here's an interesting caveat from the brine recipe for Lieutenant General Thomas "Stonewall" Jackson's barbecued ribs that comes right after instructions to add ¾ teaspoon of saltpeter: "Do not worry about the saltpeter dulling any sexual desires as this small amount has absolutely no effect on your sexual desires at all. A great deal of store bought ham, canned meats and sausages that you buy today have far more saltpeter in them than this."

Joey Keeps Puttin' on the Dog
The Nathan's Hot Dog Eating Contest, held on the Fourth of July in Coney Island, New York, was attended by more than 40,000 spectators. The event is carried live on EPSN, which has 1.949 million viewers. The 2011 event was won for the fifth time by American Joey Chestnut, who consumed 68 hot dogs WITH buns in just ten minutes flat.

Get A Long, Big Doggie
July 15, 2011 is a day that will live in hot dog infamy...that is, until someone makes one bigger. The current world-record hot dog measuring almost 670 feet long was made in Asuncion, Paraguay. The bun alone weighed 330 pounds. After the giant wiener was certified by the folks from the *Guinness World Record Book*, the dog was sliced up and eaten by the large crowd that was on hand.

Now That's a Real Whopper!
On July 3, 2011, the current world record hamburger was made at the

Alameda County Fair in California. Cooked on a 72,000-pound grill, the burger was topped with 50 pounds each of lettuce and onions and 12 pounds of pickles. The bun weighed 272 pounds and was 28 inches thick. Fair officials estimated the giant burger contained approximately 1.375 million calories, but admitted they might have been a little conservative. The local health department was on hand to make sure the meat was cooked to the proper temperature before the finished burger was weighed and certified. It then was eaten by the huge crowd that had gathered to witness the spectacle.

Burnt Ends

"Pig—let me speak his praise—is no less provocative of the appetite, than he is satisfactory to the criticalness of the palate. The strong man may batten on him, and the weakling refuseth not his mild juices [sic]."—Charles Lamb from A Dissertation Upon Roasted Pig

"No one who has had the good fortune to attend a barbecue will ever forget it. The smell of it all, the meat is slowly roasting to a delicious brown over smoking fires, the hungry and happy crowds."—Strand Magazine, London 1898

"Texas cooks, especially the male variety, will spend the whole of Sunday morning mixing, matching herbs, spices and inspiration to achieve a perfect barbecue sauce." —A Taste of Texas Cookbook, 1949 by Jane Trahey

"Texas is the place where they barbecue everything except ice cream."
—Quote from an outsider in A Taste of Texas Cookbook by Jane Trahey, 1949

"I like pigs. Dogs look up to us. Cats look down on us. Pigs treat us as equals"
—Sir Winston Churchill

General Stonewall Jackson's barbecue brine recipe called for an interesting ingredient: saltpeter.

Barbecue Trivia Stew

H ere we have collected numerous barbecue-related facts, factoids, rumors, tall tales, excuses, statistics, essentials, particulars, details, truths, falsehoods, actualities, realities, specifics, downright lies and fairy tales. Anything at all, as long has it has something to do with grilling, barbecuing, outdoor cooking, smoking, pork, beef, chicken...you get the picture.

We here at TBBQTT* (The Barbecue Think-Tank) believe this is the world's most detailed and comprehensive collection of both useful and useless information concerning outdoor cooking. This chapter on general trivia is the result of years of painstaking research. Here, you'll find information on such wide-ranging topics as barbecue rubs and sauces, the fuels for your fire, the definition of *ribfest*, and where to get your own bottle of bacon-flavored personal lubricant and massage oil. We're confident you'll soon come to realize how vital this information is to your day-to-day existence. Forget about studying the stock market or researching where to move your 401K before all of your hard earned savings fly completely out the window. Your time will be much better spent perusing these pages...and at the very least, you'll have more fun.

*TBBQTT (The Barbecue Think-Tank) is a very small tank sunk deep in the ground somewhere in the desert of Nevada, very near Area 51.

My First Barbecue Bible
Dave DeWitt, publisher of the *Fiery Foods & BBQ SuperSite*, the *Burn! Blog*, and producer of the *National Fiery Foods & BBQ Show*, describes his favorite vintage barbecue book: "Before Steven Raichlen—hell, even before James Beard—there was the original *Barbecue Bible*, but it was titled *Sunset Barbecue Book*. It was published by Lane Publishing Company of Menlo Park, California in 1938, and is believed to be the first book ever on home barbecuing. The second edition was called *Sunset Barbecue Cook Book* and published in 1950. I have, passed down from my father Dick DeWitt, the third edition, published in 1959. It cost $1.95 as a trade paperback.

Totally Q

To this day, I think it is one of the most informative books ever published on grilling and barbecue, and is one of the few books that shows you, step-by-step, how to build and use your own firepit. The chapter on smoke cooking is excellent and shows how smokers were jury-rigged long before manufactured home smokers became available. And you just don't find recipes for Spit-Roasted Calf's Liver anymore!" Sounds like this book could only be more authoritative if it were carved into stone tablets.

On Selecting Recipes For a Barbecue Cookbook
"This book is written for barbecuers of every degree of skill. Nearly every recipe within its covers was created by a charcoal chef, proudly submitted to *Sunset* magazine, and there passed through the test of fire. Each recipe was first checked over by a skeptical home economist, and if it didn't sound too outlandish, it was turned over to a veteran barbecuer to cook over charcoal. Then the acid test: the cooked delicacy was tried on a panel of suspicious folk who love barbecued meat in all its guises. Recipes that survived this ordeal were published in *Sunset* and are here assembled in book form. A glance at this assortment will show that, collectively, the barbecue chef is a nimble, versatile craftsman." —Editors of *Sunset Barbecue Cook Book*, 1959

Are You Part of the 77 Percent?
According to some sources, over 77 percent of all households in the United States own some type of an outdoor cooking device. Over half of those owners use their grills year- round, some as much as five times a month.

Are They Just Guessing?
Researchers tell us that more than 81 million Americans said they had attended a barbecue in the year 2010. My question is: *Who did they get to go around and take this survey?*

But RVs Don't Even Have Tailgates!
According to some industry analysts, approximately 25,000 RVs are rented throughout the country on a typical fall weekend for various tailgating events.

The Barbecue Capital of the World
Lexington, North Carolina calls itself "The Barbecue Capital of the World." Since 1984, the city has played host to the Lexington Barbecue Festival, one of the largest street festivals in the state. This event is famous for slow-smoked barbecued pork shoulder, served with a vinegar-based sauce on a roll. Sometimes the sandwich is topped with a red "barbecue slaw."

Totally Q

The hamburger Harley, courtesy of The Hamburger Museum.

The Hamburger Museum

In a tribute to burgers of all kinds-grilled or not-Harry Sperl of Daytona Beach, Florida has assembled more than 500 different artifacts depicting hamburgers. They include: banks, biscuit jars, clocks, hats, trays, erasers, badges, magnets, music boxes, glasses, cups, bowls, stuffed toys, calendars and postcards. The two prizes of his collection are a hamburger waterbed with a sesame seed-covered spread and matching pillows, and a Harley motorcycle customized as a giant hamburger replica. Hamburger lovers should surf on over to www.burgerweb.com for a complete description of the museum and its contents.

Thirsting for 'Cue Knowledge...Eh?

According to the website www.thebarbecuemaster.com, the country that generates the most *Google* searches regarding the immortal question, "How to barbecue chicken?" is our neighbor to the north, Canada.

Totally Q

Tools of the Trade
According to the Hearth, Patio and Barbecue Association website, the most popular barbecue utensils are: long-handled tongs (77 percent), forks (64 percent), long-handled spatulas (59 percent), and grill cleaning brushes (63 percent).

Grilling Days
The most popular holidays for barbecuing are: July Fourth (71 percent), Memorial Day (57 percent) Labor Day (55 percent).

Extremeus-Tailgatus
Many folks in the know agree that the most extreme and over-the-top tailgaters are those attending Jimmy Buffet concerts. They are reported to construct extravagant islands complete with palm trees, sand and hammocks.

Gotham City 'Cue
The Big Apple Barbecue Block Party, held each June in New York City, takes over five to six blocks of Madison Avenue for the entire weekend and features 18 pitmasters from around the country cooking their regional specialties. First held in 2002 outside the Blue Smoke Restaurant, this event now draws more than 125,000 people and has grown to include cooking demos, lectures, grilling contests, vendors and music. It's a complete barbecue extravaganza!

Caught Between a Hard Rock and a Pig Stand
A lawsuit filed in 1988 in the Lone Star State of Texas was a boondoggle for most, except of course the lawyers who, I am sure, amassed copious billable hours along the way. Texas Pig Stands v. Hard Rock Café International was initiated by a Texan named Richard Hailey, who claimed to have opened one of the very first drive-in restaurants in the country. He had an offering on his menu called a "pig sandwich," which he believed was his creation—and therefore his intellectual property.

When Hard Rock Café opened its first location in Dallas in 1986, they too, had a menu selection called—you guessed it—a "pig sandwich." This didn't sit right with Hailey, who figured he was owed a bit of compensation for what he determined was Hard Rock's infringement on his product idea.

The resulting trial included endless hours of testimony from various expert witnesses as to the origination and proliferation of pork, pork sandwiches and barbecue stands all over the country, and some courthouse regulars recalled seeing the jurors' mouths watering during parts of the testimony. The judge, while admonishing the panel to remain undisturbed and avoid news accounts of the trial over a weekend break, even

Totally Q

instructed them "not to eat any barbecue" during their time off. Talk about cruel and unusual punishment.

By now you're undoubtedly curious as to the outcome. Well, it was a difficult and contentious ruling, but the jury upheld Texas Pig Stands' claim that Hard Rock had infringed on their trademark. They didn't, however, go so far as to award a cut of the profits, but instead limited the amount to $400,000 for legal fees. This judgment was subsequently reversed during a 1992 appeal.

Shouldn't Pork Butt Be Bringing Up the Rear?
The most popular foods Americans grill, in order of preference are: hamburgers, steak and hot dogs, with chicken breasts bringing up the rear.

A Pigot by Any Other Name is Still a Pigot
We have all heard of a bigot, and most of us are aware of its meaning. In *America's Best BBQ* by Ardie Davis and Paul Kirk, however, a definition appears for the newest word to be added to the English language via the barbecue world. "Pigot: An individual who is hogmatic, i.e., believes that the only true barbecue is pig barbecue: usually exhibits other hogmatic beliefs and behaviors [sic]."

Carbecue: Driving Under the Influence of 'Cue
When most people hear the word *carbecue*, their thoughts are taken immediately to the term coined by a corny FM drive time traffic reporter who was describing a car that had caught fire and was causing traffic backups along a commuter route.

Well folks, *carbecue* really exists as a culinary technique; in fact, I stumbled upon an entire process for preparing a meal on the engine of your car at www.wikihow.com/ Cook-Food-on-Your-Car's-Engine! The article leads with: "Nothing puts a damper on a road trip like having to stop the car, pop the hood, and check the engine—unless of course you're just checking to see if your pork tenderloin is done. Engine-block cooking is a tradition going back almost as long as the automobile itself, and now that gasoline prices are at an all-time high, it's never made more sense to ask your engine to do more than just get you from point A to point B. Start your engines and get ready to carbecue!"

On the site you'll find detailed instructions on how to turn your vehicle into a rolling slow cooker, including a handy distance chart that can be printed and taped onto your sun visor for quick reference:
- Shrimp: 30-50 miles
- Trout or salmon: 60-100 miles

Totally Q

- Chicken breasts: 60 miles at 65 mph
- Chicken wings: 140-200 miles
- Pork tenderloin: 250 miles
- Sliced, peeled potatoes: 55 miles

The article also includes some helpful tips and warnings that have become a part of everyday life here in today's extremely litigious society, including: "Turn off the engine before opening the hood. To avoid serious injury, don't try to place, check, or remove your food with the engine running." It additionally advises folks to think twice before attempting to brew a stew in this manner, noting that foods with a lot of liquid could be messy and harmful to the engine.

Why the "Wall" in Wall Street?

Way back when our country was only the thirteen original colonies, the wild pig population was increasing rapidly, which causes me to believe that portable pig roasters and community pig pickings had yet to become popular. There were so many hogs running loose in the New York City area, in fact, that a wall was constructed just to keep them out, and the structure remained in place for so long that a street was eventually built alongside it. Locals in the area labeled the road—by now I am sure you're way ahead of me here—Wall Street. "The Street" still boasts a subtle barbecue influence, which is known by only a few of New York's tight-knit barbecue community. While many of the uninformed believe that Wall Street's famous bull statue is supposed to symbolize the "bullish" stock market, real Gotham City insiders know that the bronze bovine actually symbolizes brisket as the hardest piece of beef to barbecue. We all know there are still plenty of swine to be found working on Wall Street, so I guess the wall wasn't completely effective.

Will The Real Bozo Please Shut Up and Cook?

Bozo's Hot Pit Bar-B-Que was opened in 1923 just northeast of Memphis, Tennessee by Thomas "Bozo" Williams. Things were cruising along pretty well for the establishment

Totally Q

until 1982, when Bozo's daughter, Helen Williams, filed for a trademark to ensure that no other restaurant could use the name.

This didn't sit right with one Larry Harmon, who was known to many kids as the original "Bozo the Clown." Mr. Harmon had registered the moniker as an entertainer but not as a restaurant, and as a result, Bozo the Clown challenged Bozo the barbecuer for sole use of the name. Enter the other bozos (in the form of the lawyers), who were probably laughing all the way to the bank on this one. A 1991 *New York Times* article reported that, at the time, more than $150,000 in legal fees had piled up. I can just see the itemized bill now:

Instruct secretary: 3 minutes

Take phone call from client: 8 minutes

Eat pulled pork sandwich: 15 minutes

Adjust red squeaking nose and pointed orange hair for court appearance: 10 minutes

Shine extremely large shoes: 25 minutes

Can anyone say *cha-ching*? The restaurant ultimately won, but only after the case went all the way to the U.S. Supreme Court.

What Does "Livin' High on the Hog" Actually Mean?

We've all heard this expression, but do we really know what it means? My research resulted in a fairly simple definition: to be very comfortable or well-off. So well-off, in fact, that you are able to afford the highest cuts of meat from the hog, the loin cuts, which are more prized than the leg or shoulder areas.

Here are a few more definitions as provided by everyone's favorite know-it-all, the *Merriam-Webster* dictionary:

Hog wild: Lacking in restraint of judgment or temper. We all know someone who fits this bill.

Hog tie: To tie the front feet together.

Hog-wash: Swill, slop, balderdash. You've gotta love it when anyone uses the word *balderdash*.

Hog-score: A line used in curling seven yards from the tee, also known as **hog-line.** Curling...and they say competition barbecue isn't a sport.

Hogs-head: A large cask or barrel.

Hogmanay: The eve of New Year's Day.

Hog heaven: An extremely satisfying state or situation.

49

Totally Q

Hog-back: A ridge of land formed by the outcropping edges of tilted strata, not to be confused with a broke back.

Whole hog: Committed without reservation, the whole way, the farthest limit, completely in.

To further illustrate the creative use of these terms, here is a short swine story: "It was Hogmanay back in 1979. I was livin' high on the hog up on Hog Back Mountain when I decided to go whole hog and consume a hogs-head full of hog-wash liquor, which caused me to go hog wild and get arrested. The cops had to hog tie me, as I thought I was in hog heaven while standing on the hog-line of my neighbor's curling court." *Curling...does he really call that a sport?*

BBQ with a Sterling Reputation
One of the now-famous three tenors, Luciano Pavarotti, was allegedly a big (and I mean BIG) fan of Carolina pork barbecue. It is reported that back in 2002, he requested and was served some tasty barbecue after a performance in the city of Raleigh, North Carolina. The twist was, his 'cue was served in a silver bowl.

Got What?
The wording below is on the back of the T-shirt for the Pavone Brothers BBQ Team from Virginia:

Legs

Thighs

Butts

Breasts

Got Wood?

Every time I wear this shirt, I get a few laughs. And no, it's not because they see a triple X guy in a single X shirt. That's my story and I am sticking to it.

Americans Go For the Dogs
Americans eat approximately 20 billion hot dogs a year, which averages out to around 70 hot dogs per person. Of that total number, 15 percent are sold by street vendors and 9 percent are eaten at ballparks. In addition, dogs are served in 95 percent of the homes across the country. Wow, pass the mustard.

Too Many Dogs, Not Enough Buns
Did you ever wonder why there are 10 hot dogs per pack and only eight hot dog rolls

in a bag? It makes no sense. Someone ought to do something about this problem! Why hasn't Congress addressed this issue? Where's the grand jury investigation? The answer boils down to stubbornness...are you surprised?

When hot dogs were first offered to the public they were sold loose. It wasn't until 1940 that they began to be sold in packs of 10 and today, most dogs are still offered this way. Although most bakeries still stick to the "pack of eight" for hot dog rolls, some are starting to relent and now sell 10 rolls to a pack. Finally, someone is thinking. In general, however, both sides are very reluctant to move, but know that some adjustment is needed to avoid legions of frustrated hot dog eaters moving over to tofu dogs, which, sources tell me, are offered in packs of eight.

The Original Ph.B. or Doctor of Barbecue Philosophy

Ardie Davis, a.k.a. Remus Powers, Ph.B., is a real barbecue man from Kansas City. He took on the name *Remus Powers* while writing for the school newspaper in college, where he majored in philosophy,, choosing *Remus* for the Joel Chandler Harris tales he read as a child (and still enjoys today), and *Powers* for a mechanic in the shop where his father worked. Today, this character is well-known for his outfit that includes a derby hat, tuxedo shirt, bow tie and butcher's apron.

Over the years, Ardie has done much to promote barbecue both as a cuisine and a form of entertainment for the whole family , writing several barbecue cookbooks and contributing as a regular columnist for the *KCBS Bullsheet* and the *National Barbecue News*.

Remus Powers, Ph.B. Photo courtesy KCBS

In 1984, Ardie was beating the bushes for some additional credibility to bestow on his fictitious character Remus Powers, which by then had evolved into his barbecue persona. He thought the designation of Ph.B., (Doctor of Barbecue Philosophy), sounded impressive and important, so he made the declaration.

Totally Q

As interest in the Ph.B. accreditation grew, Ardie and a few of the early members of this elite fraternity formed a committee of sorts to oversee the requirements and applications for those deemed worthy of this honor and then created the fictitious Greasehouse University as the source for this most prestigious of degrees. Since that time, the Ph.B. has become one of the most sought-after sheepskins of its kind...right up there with the Doctorate of Love Degree.

Town Names that Make Me Want to Fire Up the Grill

Burnt Corn, Alabama
Hog Jaw, Arkansas
Weiner, Arkansas
Burnt Ranch, California
Hambone, California
Hogtown, California
Black Hog Landing, Delaware
Beer Bottle Crossing, Idaho
Gnaw Bone, Indiana
Hog Back, Kansas
Chicken Bristle, Kentucky
Belcher, Louisiana
Cow Yard, Massachusetts
Hog Heaven, Montana

Upper Pig Pen, North Carolina
Pigeye, Ohio
Hogshooter, Okalahoma
Beersville, Pennsylvania
Chicken Town, Pennsylvania
Pigs Ear, Pennsylvania
Smoketown, Pennsylvania
Cow Head Landing, South Carolina
Cow Tail, South Carolina
Marrowbone, Tennessee
Smoke Rise, Tennessee
Bean Station, Texas
Lick Skillet, Virginia
Hog Eye, West Virginia

25,000 Chicken Dinners...In a Single Day?

The Sertoma Club of Lancaster has been having their annual barbecued chicken dinner on the third Saturday in May since 1953. This yardbird feast is the club's largest fundraiser for the whole year and has grown so much that it is now recognized by the *Guinness Book of World Records* as the largest one-day chicken barbecue, preparing and serving more than 25,000 complete chicken dinners. They even have drive-thru lines for folks in a rush to git their chicken and split.

Crazy Products Inspired by BBQ & Smoked Meat

Bacon Flavored Soda

Soda flavored with bacon was introduced in 2010 by J&D Foods, partnered with Jones Soda. The product was released in time for the 2010 holiday season and offered in a bacon-themed gift bag. For ten bucks you could get two bottles of bacon soda, a bag of cheddar and bacon-flavored popcorn, a tube of bacon-infused lip balm and a package of bacon-flavored country gravy mix. Bacon soda was the brainchild of the same two guys who introduced the infamous turkey and gravy soda, just a few years before. Further research revealed that they have made and attempted to distribute a multitude of meat-based beverages including flavors such as: cheeseburger, chicken teriyaki, buffalo wings, fish 'n' chips, and fried oysters. They even created a breakfast drink that combined the flavors of bacon, eggs and buttered toast.

Make Mine a Bacontini

Just when you think you have heard it all, they come out with something that makes you sit up and take notice. Bacon-flavored vodka has been available since 2009 from a Seattle, Washington-based company named Black Rock Spirits. Their Bakon Vodka is just what you need to make a bacon bloody Mary or bacon martini.

Darling, You Smell Just Like...Barbecue?

Here's the gift that every woman secretly longs...nay, lusts...for. Que Eau De Barbeque is authentic barbecue-scented cologne. No, I am not making this up. This fragrance is the brainchild of Brett Thompson and Heath Hall, the founders of Pork Barrel BBQ out of Washington, D.C.

According to their website at www. porkbarrelbbq.com: "Que, an intoxicating bouquet of spices, smoke, meat, and sweet summer sweat, is the latest development in wearable scents and is quickly becoming a hit among meat lovers, grill masters, and backyard BBQ'ers. Recognizing the absence of a barbeque-scented cologne and perfume, Pork Barrel BBQ worked with a team of craftsmen and fine perfumers to create the perfect barbeque aroma. Until now, no fragrance manufacturer has ever succeeded in bottling the intoxicating scents associated with barbeque and its mixture of spices, smoke and meat." I don't know about you, but I've really been wishing for a scent that features "sweet summer sweat." Come to think of it, I wouldn't even need to wear the cologne three months out of the year!

Lovin' that Barbecue Sauce Loaf

This deli meat selection is very popular in the Baltimore area. I spent a considerable amount of time searching the Net to find out what it is or how the product is made, but so far, I have nothing. What I can tell you is what's on the label: "Barbecue Sauce Loaf, covered with pork fat, paprika and spice." Under "ingredients" we have pork, water, beef, calcium reduced dried skim milk, salt, sugar, dextrose, flavorings, dehydrated tomatoes, dehydrated onions and garlic, sodium phosphate, monosodium glutamate, spices, vinegar, sodium erythorbate (my personal favorite), vegetable oil, oleoresin of paprika, sodium nitrate, and hydrolyzed soy and corn protein. Yum!

Be a bacon *lover*
www.baconlube.com

Perhaps Some Things *Shouldn't* Taste Like Bacon

Yes folks, you can now buy bacon-flavored rolling papers, and they are available on Amazon. Talk about convenience—you can twist one up, smoke it, and cure the munchies all at the same time. What will they think of next? Well, I think I answered my own question, and I'm still shaking my head after reading about Baconlube, which is billed to be "the world's first bacon-flavored personal lubricant and massage oil." Check out the website at www.baconlube.com, because this is something you really need to see in order to believe.

What's Next...Bacon Deodorant?

Bacon air fresheners—what else can I say? Barbecue Nirvana. This product is an absolute must for your barbecue-mobile.

I'll Have a Double Dip of BBQ

An ice cream store in Rehoboth Beach, Delaware was the first to introduce barbecue-flavored ice cream. The concoction was the brainchild of Chip Hearn, owner of the Udder Delight Ice Cream House, and Peppers, the world-famous Rehoboth Beach-based hot sauce shop. Word on the street is that the ice cream flavor was not a success. Back to the drawing board, I guess.

Totally Q

A BBQ Prayer

"Dear Lord, we thank you for these barbecue ribs and beef we're about to eat, and bless the cow that they come from. You know Lord, we're grateful for most of your animals, except those that get themselves killed on the highway and wind up being eaten by the vultures. Heck Lord, if it weren't for barbecue all we'd have is chili and you know a man can't live on that stuff forever! So we're thankful Lord, even if we forget to say so, for this barbecue we're about to eat. Amen!" —Courtesy of Big O's Barbecue Fun Facts at www.bigosbbq.com

The Barbecue Rules

When a man volunteers to do the barbecue, the following chain of events is put into motion (courtesy of www.funny2.com):

(1) The woman buys the food.

(2) The woman makes the salad, prepares the vegetables and makes dessert.

(3) The woman prepares the meat for cooking, places it on a tray along with the necessary cooking utensils and sauces and takes it to the man (who is lounging beside the grill, beer in hand).

(4) The woman remains outside the compulsory three-meter exclusion zone where the exuberance of testosterone and other manly bonding activities can take place without the interference of the woman.

Here comes the important part:

(5) THE MAN PLACES THE MEAT ON THE GRILL.

More routine...

(6) The woman goes inside to organize the plates and cutlery.

(7) The woman comes out to tell the man that the meat is looking great. He thanks her and asks if she will bring another beer while he flips the meat.

Important again:

(8) THE MAN TAKES THE MEAT OFF THE GRILL AND HANDS IT TO THE WOMAN.

More routine...

(9) The woman prepares the plates, salad, bread, utensils, napkins and sauces, then brings them to the table.

(10) After eating, the woman clears the table and does the dishes.

And most important of all:

(11) Everyone PRAISES the MAN and THANKS HIM for his cooking efforts.

(12) The man asks the woman how she enjoyed "her night off " and, upon seeing her annoyed reaction, concludes that there's just no pleasing some women.

Totally Q

Vegetarian Ribs? You Have Got to Be Kidding

In 1986 after considerable pressure from various vegetarian groups, contest organizer Mike Royko relented and permitted several vegan groups to submit entries in his annual Ribfest. Royko compared the taste and texture of the submissions to that of rubber and thought that there was a possible market for the products due to the large number of people who regularly chewed on pencil erasers. Mike insisted he had nothing personal against those who prefer veggies to meat, telling a reporter, "I occasionally eat vegetables—a tiny onion in a martini or a stalk of celery in a bloody Mary keeps me fit."

Awaken the Woman's Barbecual Desire!

This from *The Man's Book of the BBQ* by Brendan McGinley: "Brother, you've got to have dames. The things we love about barbecue are the qualities we love in woman: fundamentally sweet with a smoky air, just a touch of saltiness for character, and the hotter the better. A man's biological role is to bring back sustenance for the clan. In providing lush delicacies to your loved ones, you're satisfying your hunter genes so that your chosen mates (and let's face it, you're not picky) will survive to bear children. That instinct cuts both ways. Someone who enjoys and indulges in life's joys is far more attractive than a bore who cuts a good figure. That's why a rich and handsome champion like Tom Brady has never seduced any of the women you or I have loved. Wake the gustatory pleasure of a woman's barbecual desire, and you'll be awash in her orange, greasy kisses."

The Guys at Gonehoggin' Started Early

The Gonehoggin' competition barbecue team from Bear, Delaware flies a banner at contests that says, "Pullin' our pork since the third grade." After reading this I thought: *Gee, that's an awful young age to be barbecuing.*

The Great American Barbecue Novel

Barbecue contests have been the setting for several works of fiction over the years. Here are a few of those selections:

Thin Blue Smoke by Doug Worgul, Burnside Books, 2012: A story about love, second chances, despair and redemption in a fictional Kansas City barbecue joint.

Totally Q

Baptists at our Barbecue by Robert F Smith: This is a book about a mountain town located in the southwest that has an ongoing dispute between the Mormons and Baptists. I am not really sure where the barbecue fits in, but it was in the title so I felt obliged to add it to the list.

Stiffs and Swine by J. B. Stanley, Llewellyn Worldwide Publishers, 2008: A barbecued who-done-it? in which a contestant is found dead at a barbecue contest.

Finger Lickin' Fifteen by Janet Evanovich: This is the 15th book of the Stephanie Plum mystery series surrounding the murder of a TV celebrity chef who was in town to promote a barbecue contest.

Murder at the Blue Ridge Barbecue Festival by Gene Davis: Another murder mystery set at a barbecue festival. I think I am noticing a pattern here.

Memphis Ribs by Gerald Duff, Salvo Press: A murder mystery, but this time, not set at a barbecue contest. The lead detective on the case, however, is a firm believer in the redemptive powers of barbecued pork.

Revenge of the Barbecue Queens by Lou Jane Temple, Macmillan Publishers, 1997: Pigpen Hopkins is one of the favored cooks in the barbecue World Series. That is, until he is found stuck into a pot of his super-secret barbecue sauce. And here I thought all barbecuers were nice and friendly people.

Jack and the Giant Barbecue by Eric Kimmel: A kid book that is a twist on the classic fairy tale, *Jack and the Beanstalk*.

The Politics of Barbecue by Blake Fontenay, John F. Blair publisher: A newly released novel, this is a story about Pete Pigg, proprietor of The Pigg Pen tavern, who gets himself elected Mayor of Memphis. His plan is to build the Barbecue Hall of Fame and the plot centers around the associated greed and corruption that is all-too-familiar these days in the world of politics.

Bacon Band-Aids For Your BBQ Boo-boos

Here's a must-have addition to your grilling first-aid kit: Band-Aids shaped like pieces of bacon. If they also had the smell of bacon, I can imagine there would be a large increase in guys going to the nurse's office for a bandage. Wait a minute! Bacon-scented and -shaped bandages, girls in nurses' uniforms...sounds like the prequel to a soft porn movie. Not that I know anything about such, er, disgusting productions.

Totally Q

Barbecue Symbolism in The South
Food writer Laura Dove described the important role of barbecue down South: "Aside from its succulent taste, delicious sauces and the inimitable, smoky atmosphere of an authentic barbecue joint, barbecue has become a Southern icon, a symbol that is cherished by Southerners. Without the racist subtext of the Stars and Bars, the anachronistic sexism of the Southern belle, or the bland ennui of a plate of grits, barbecue has become a cultural icon for Southerners, of every race, class and sex."

The Politically Correct Southern Pig
"...only in the South does the slow cooking of meat over the smoke of hardwood embers assume a level of ritual and tradition usually associated with Masonic orders. John Shelton Reed, a professional Dixieologist at the University of North Carolina, put it well when he suggested that since the Rebel flag had become too controversial, we replace it with a symbol that all Southerners could support: a neon pig." —Jim Auchmutey

High-Calibre Rib Rub Technique
Vince Staten and Greg Johnson have written a must-have book for anyone interested in barbecue and barbecue joints: *Real Barbecue, the Classic Barbecue Guide to the Best Joints Across the USA.* This book is not only filled with a ton of great places to find good barbecue, but it also has a very nice collection of "porklore," which is like folklore, only with a barbecue twist, and one such story had me wondering: *Why didn't I think of that?*

Seems the authors asked one of their buddies to load a few shotgun shells with barbecue rub instead of pellets, then they hung some ribs from a tree in their backyard and commenced to firing. The plan was to infuse, by way of extreme force, the barbecue rub into the meat. Additionally, they thought, the process would serve as sort of a 'high brass' way of tenderizing their ribs. After it was all over, however, they found that the results weren't quite what they had anticipated: The ribs appeared and tasted no different than when the rub was applied in a more traditional way (not much fun there). They also noted that their experiment had done little else other than scare the next door neighbor out of her wits.

Somebody Give This Guy a Ph.B.
The year was 1981 and John Marshall, a student at Western Kentucky University, was working on his master's thesis titled *Barbecue in Western Kentucky: An Ethnographic Study.* The title alone gives me a slight headache. What follows is a short synopsis of Mr. Marshall's work: "After briefly placing barbeque cookery in its proper historical

perspective as a traditional method of food preparation, this study describes from an ethnographic viewpoint the methodologies and attitudes of two traditional barbecue cooks, Rev. E. J. Jones of Columbus, Kentucky, and Woody Smith of Arlington, Kentucky, the commercial establishments in which they cook and the role of this form of folk cookery in the area in which these men are located. This material is then utilized to draw conclusions based on the changes which have occurred in the form, process and function of barbecue in the transition from the traditional to the commercial and to indicate the effects these changes might have on the foodways of Western Kentuckians."

Now in the spirit of full disclosure, I hold neither a master's nor a doctorate in anything at all, except maybe my unofficial Doctorate of Stoogeology: The Study of The Three Stooges and Stooge-Related Issues. While I'm very sure the paper is probably very insightful, informative and thought provoking, I'm thinking Mr. Marshall needs to spend a little more time with a slow-burning fire and a little less time with his word processor. I suppose back in 1981 it was a typewriter, but you get my drift.

I Read it On My BBQ Apron
Aprons worn by barbecue cooks have become integral parts of their repertoire. That being said, the creators and manufactures of these accessories have taken the common cook's cover-up to new heights (or perhaps depths) with their clever wording. Here are a few of my favorites:

Save the vegetables, eat more sausage

OK, if it makes you happy call the fire department

This grill ain't big enough for both of us

How do you like your steak burnt?

The ladies love my thick meat

If it ain't barbecue it ain't food

Bloody or burnt?

If I'm on fire this is not a training exercise (please extinguish)

Kill a cow, start a fire, the magic begins

I didn't claw my way up the food chain just to eat vegetables

Vegetarian is an Indian word meaning "Bad Hunter"

Totally Q

Never trust a skinny chef

I love animals (especially in a good gravy)

Real Men don't use recipes

I'd tell you the recipe but then I'd have to kill you

This Guru Doesn't Wear a Turban

The BBQ Guru was introduced in 2004 as the first-ever barbecue cooker electric temperature control device. It was created by Fred Pirkle (1946-2012) of Therm-Omega-Tech, Inc. of Warminster, Pennsylvania, a company known throughout the world for manufacturing temperature control devices. "Shotgun Fred" (as he was affectionately known around the competition barbecue circuit) held many patents for temperature control devices and valves used in everything from factory machinery to locomotives. I was fortunate to have spent an evening or two with Shotgun, sharing a cold drink around a competition campfire. He was a humble and humorous guy who just loved to cook outdoors, and it showed in his enthusiasm for his creations.

Many discussions have been held over the years as to which changes and/or improvements have had the greatest influence on barbecue and outdoor cooking in recent years, and it's my humble opinion that the Guru temperature control device has to be at the top of the list. With this unit, pitmasters can "set it and forget it," which allows them time away from their cookers. The Guru also results in a more even temperature within the cooking chamber, which translates to a better- finished product. The unit is adaptable to most commercially-available smokers and barbecue cookers.

Carolina 'Cue Attacked!

"Barbecue in the Carolinas almost always takes the form of chopped meat sandwiches. By the time the meat and sometimes the fat and skin have been minced together and smothered with sauce, the taste of the barbecue has been so masked as to make it difficult to tell how the meat was prepared. But if the meat is the main attraction and the sauce merely an enhancement, this technique defeats the entire purpose of barbecue." —Lolis Eric Ellie

Tailgating Trivia

Game...There's a Game?

Reports from (I am not making this stuff up) the American Tailgaters Association indicate that approximately 30 percent of tailgaters never see the inside of the stadium.

Totally Q

The Largest Tailgate Party of the Year
The Florida-Georgia collegiate football game in Jacksonville, Florida is reported to be the largest tailgating event of the year. In fact, some fans begin arriving on Wednesday before the Saturday game and many stay over, delaying their departure until sometime on Sunday.

The "Typical Tailgater"
I had no idea there was such a thing as a "typical tailgater," but here' a description of one, straight from www.tailgating.com (a website run by Joe Cahn, the self-described Commissioner of Tailgating:)

- College-educated male.
- Between the ages of 35 and 44.
- Spends over $500 a year on tailgating food.
- Attends and/or hosts 6-10 tailgate parties each season.
- Uses separate coolers for food and beverages.
- Travels less than one hour to get to the game.
- Begins tailgate party 3-4 hours before kickoff.

Top Tailgating Cities
According to a 2007 survey by www.hightechtailgating.com, the top five U.S. cities for tailgating enthusiasm are as follows:

1 Baltimore
2. Denver
3. Houston
4. San Diego
5. Cincinnati

Burnt Ends

"Life is too short for a half-rack."
—Mike Mills, author of *Peace, Love, and Barbecue*, Murphysboro, IL

"Barbecue, like martial arts, developed everywhere in a variety of styles. Different times call for different men, and the stalwart grillmeister heeds his destiny without regard to secondary, earthly affairs like paying rent or acknowledging his offspring. —*The Man's Book of BBQ* by Brendan McGinley

Totally Q

"Men like to barbecue. Men will cook if danger is involved." —Comic Rita Rudner

"Food has replaced sex in my life—now I can't even get into my own pants." —Comic Lynda Montgomery

"The only time to eat diet food is while you're waiting for the steak to cook." —Julia Child

"I didn't fight my way to the top of the food chain to be a vegetarian." —Erma Bombeck

"I'm at the age where food has taken the place of sex. In fact, I just had a mirror put over my kitchen table." —Rodney Dangerfield
"All depends who you're having sex with, or whose barbecue you're eating." — Barbecue cook Cheryl Litman, when asked if barbecue is better than sex

"If it weren't for BBQ-ing, I'd have no reason to have a backyard." —Willy Hawk in *The Marlboro Cook Like a Man Cookbook*

"Barbecue starts around midnight when the men get the hickory logs going...There are always two sauces, one for the meat and one for the cook."—Merle Ellis

"If you don't take cooking seriously you're not going to make anything tasty. A barbecue might seem like the best place to just sit back and enjoy some good food and drinks, but if you don't respect the fact that there's a right way to do this, your food is never going to come out right." —Myron Mixon

"Did you ever see the customers in health food stores? They are pale, skinny people who look half dead. In a steak house, you see robust, ruddy people. They're dying of course, but they look terrific." —Bill Cosby

"I found there was only one way to look thin: hang out with fat people." —Rodney Dangerfield

"Whether you're a grilling novice or an experienced home chef, it's important to know that great grilled, barbecued, and smoked foods are about timing and temperature." —Barry "CB" Martin

"They say sharing your secret barbeque recipe with another person is like sharing your wife with another man—nothing good ever comes from it." —"Famous Dave" Anderson

Politics and Barbecue

B arbecue and politics are almost natural bedfellows; they go together like peas and carrots. In the early years of our country's political history, politicians, as well as those aspiring to hold public office, oftentimes used barbecue in their quest to become "servants of the public" (said, of course, with dripping sarcasm).

In the days before television and the 24-hour news cycle, folks seeking to earn or stay in public office often would host large picnics or barbecues as a way to draw big crowds. Once the crowds were assembled, the attendees filled their bellies with free barbecued meats which were frequently washed down with free beer and other inhibition-lowering drinks. After the feed, the politicos would commence to bore...I mean to inform...the constituency of the benefits they would receive simply by voting for them. To me, it wasn't a bad tradeoff for listening to a political speech, which for the most part, is made up of a lot of lies along with a smattering of false promises.

Of course I think I need to quantify the word *free* when used to describe the political gatherings of yesteryear. It is a well-known fact that politicians love to extol the virtues of being very thrifty when it comes to taxpayers' monies. It is also a more than well-known fact that these same leaders specialize, excel and rejoice in the spending of someone else's money (as opposed to their own). As such, I am quite sure that even those gatherings held before Al Gore invented the Internet were paid for or funded by someone looking to exchange a donation for a favor or two or three. Truth is, not that much has changed in the 200 or so years we have been a country. Nepotism, crony- ism and payola are still as alive today as they were in the early days. Only the names and faces have changed—and in some cases, the names haven't changed at all.

What has changed, however, is that old-time politicians needed to gather a crowd to get their message out. Today's political message has been reduced to the 20- or 30- second sound bite read from a teleprompter, with a small, yet enthusiastic and diverse crowd (along with a few American flags) in the background. This is attributed partly to the fact that an average person's attention span these days is no longer than a

Totally Q

gnat's, and partly to the proliferation of the 24-hour news cycle. Today, armed with the right connections and a few well-placed contributions, almost anyone can get

themselves some air time on any of the multitude of news stations located on the cable or satellite dial as these broadcast venues need something to fill the voids between the commercials, teasers and film clips of the latest police chase.

While I don't believe that today's political leaders are much different than our forefathers, I do believe that something is missing

An old Virginia barbecue scene.

and a bit out of whack in today's political theater. Gone are the days when the politicians were grateful for votes and expressed their gratitude by feeding the masses. The free barbecues of bygone campaigns have been replaced by the modern-day political fundraiser. In the past, politicians picked up the bill for our slow-smoked barbecued meats and afterwards bored us with their speechifying. Contrast that to today, when folks plop down thousands of dollars per plate just to eat rubber chicken, rub elbows with elected officials, and THEN be bored out of their minds with false promises and bravado.

Barbecue Villains, Candidates, or Constituents?

"Barbecue! For one day at least, leave toil behind and eat your fill of hog meat and beef! Get yourself good and drunk without spending a dime! Sing, reel and dance to the fiddle! Revel with friends! Laugh with the politician who donated the meat! Assure him that you would not be so rude as to vote for another man! Stay steady for the stump speeches ahead! Do not get so drunk as to disgrace the republic! Give in to some temptations! Resist others! Steer clear of those James Kirke Paulding called, 'roysterers, tosspots and barbecue villains,' who in merriment or crime ply you with rotgut. Remember who you are! Remember why you are here! Remember that, however humble your beginnings. Here you stand, enfranchised, a man of status in this new world!" —Fletcher W. Green, from *Savage Barbecue*

Totally Q

Guns, Booze, and Spiel

In the book Ante-Bellum North Carolina, Guion Johnson gave a firsthand account of what went on at the political barbecues held in the early days of our country: "Eating barbecued meat, drinking toasts, discharging firearms and listening to orations by politicians and local dignitaries." The combination of firearms and alcohol is a definite no-no, but when you throw politicians into the mix...well, it's a surprise anyone survived to get elected.

In the nineteenth century, barbecue was a feature at church picnics and political rallies as well as at private parties. A barbecue was a popular and relatively inexpensive way to lobby for votes, and the organizers of political rallies would provide barbecue, lemonade, and usually a bit of whiskey. These gatherings were also an easy way for different classes to mix. Barbecue was not a class-specific food, and large groups of people from every stratum could mix to eat, drink and listen to stump speeches. Journalist Jonathan Daniels, writing in the mid-twentieth century, maintained that, 'Barbecue is the dish which binds together the taste of both the people of the big house and the poorest occupants of the back end of the broken-down barn.' –Laura Dove

"George, What Have You Done?"

Historians to this day come down on both sides of the discussion surrounding the question as to whether George Washington, the Father of Our Country, actually chopped down a cherry tree and then was honest when asked about his deed back in 1738. What is NOT in dispute, but is known only to a select few, was what George was planning to do with that cherry tree, as well as some peach and pecan wood he had collected from the neighborhood. You see, George and several of his Mount Vernon buddies had constructed a smoker out in the woods behind George's house. They used their smoker to slow-roast much of the wild game they harvested from the woods and streams in the area. Some scholars believe that, while young GW may have owned up to ending the life of the cherry tree in his father's garden, he neglected to mention the other fruitwood tress he and his buddies had sacrificed in their quest for the perfect 'cue. Some say if you search around in the area, you can find a brass plaque overgrown with weeds, inscribed with these not-so-famous words, "George Washington smoked here."

The Origin of "Pork Barrel" Politics

We've all heard the term "pork barrel politics." It seems like just about every news story coming out of Washington has at least a mention of the term. My question is this: What did the swine family ever do to deserve such a negative association? It's a widely known fact that our friends the pigs like to wallow in slop and root in the ground looking for acorns, and some would argue that this behavior is very similar in

Totally Q

nature to our elected representatives who like to wallow in—well let's be honest here, cash—and root for more cash, no matter what the cost. As far as I'm concerned, the similarities stop there, and the pig is the offended party.

The term actually had its origin back in the 1800s, when it was used to describe any and all spending by politicians to benefit the constituency. Originally, the term did not have the negative connotation of today: A barrel of salt pork was a common food item in 19th century households, and a family that was doing well usually had one on hand.

It wasn't until after the Civil War that the term began to take on a negative spin, much to the chagrin of hogs everywhere. Through a series of public opinion polls, the folks in Washington determined it was more important to create spending bills and pork barrel projects than it was to listen to what the folks at home were saying. "Budgets? We don't need no stinkin' budgets!" became the mantra of many on the Hill. Let the rooting and wallowing begin!

The World's Largest BBQ Party
When the mayor of Oklahoma City, John C. "Jack" Walton, ran for governor in 1922, he made a promise. Back then, when politicos made promises, sometimes they kept them. This of course, is totally different than today. He told his constituency that, if elected, he would throw an old-fashioned barbecue and invite the entire state. Well, he won the election (my guess is because the voters REALLY liked barbecue), and the best part is, he kept his promise.

Walton recruited a couple of producers of Wild West shows to help him get organized, and one of his first official directives was to issue a proclamation stating that there would be no waltzing or other highbrow-type dancing at his celebration. Only the two step, square dancing, reels and other western-style hoedown dances would be permitted. He had the members of his cabinet (along with other high-ranking party officials) comb the countryside looking for musicians to provide entertainment. The state carpenters set about flooring the center area of a half-mile racetrack to create a dance floor.

Things were really coming together for the event, which was held January 10-11, 1923. The governor-elect issued a call to all Oklahoma farmers for enough meat to serve more than 200,000 people and they responded by producing thousands of cattle, hogs, sheep and chickens. Additionally, folks donated "103 turkeys, 1,363 rabbits, 26 squirrels, 134 opossums, 113 geese, 15 deer, 2 buffalo, and 2 reindeer." As I read over the list, the most surprising missing ingredient for this four-star political

Totally Q

gathering was the barrels of pork fat. My guess is they just forgot to add them to the list, as I'm sure they were plentiful.

Large pits were constructed, totaling over a mile of trenches and more than 500 butchers were brought in for the day. They even had gigantic coffee percolators constructed; some say they were the size of railroad cars, each able to brew over 10,000 gallons of joe. Although it cannot be confirmed, my guess is that the newly elected governor's cousin got the coffee pot building contract; after all, we are talking about politicians here, aren't we?

Log Cabins and Hard Cider
President William Henry Harrison served only 30 days in office before succumbing to pneumonia in 1841, and holds the record for the shortest presidential term in American history. What is not quite as widely known is that Harrison, his running mate John Tyler and other members of the Whig party were notorious for finding ways to convince voters to support their causes and candidates. In fact, Harrison was known as the "log cabin and hard cider candidate" because his campaign held huge picnics and barbecues, during which supporters handed out liquor in small bottles shaped like log cabins, made just for the campaign. One barbecue in Bowling Green, Kentucky went a step further by featuring a miniature log cabin constructed by James Murrell. The small building was pulled to the event by six white stallions, all of which were festooned with flags, banners and other assorted campaign paraphernalia. Some years later, Samuel Eliot Morrison characterized Harrison's tactics as "the jolliest and most idiotic presidential campaign in our history." He went on to say, "the Whigs beat the Democrats by their own methods. They adopted no platform, nominated a military hero, ignored real issues, and appealed to the emotions rather than the brains of the voters." Kind of gives new meaning to the old phrase, "The more things change, the more they stay the same," doesn't it?

Totally Q

Ike Liked to Kill It and Cook It

Most people know that Eisenhower was an army general before he was the president from 1953 to 1961. What a lot of people don't know, however, was that Ike was an avid outdoorsman, a proficient marksman, an archer and an accomplished outdoor cook. Many a summer evening would find him on the roof of the White House, grilling steaks or spinning a chicken on his charcoal rotisserie. He also was known to cook in the presidential solarium and when asked by an inquiring reporter about how he got the smoke out of that room, he replied, "By opening the windows."

President Eisenhower flipping steaks with Herbert Hoover in Colorado, 1954.

Ike also loved to hunt and fish and used Camp David in Maryland's Catoctin Mountains for more than a place to be photographed walking down a leaf-strewn path while chatting with another world leader. Often, he would go out into the woods to search for game–imagine that! Included in the 1990 book Ike the Cook are some of this president's favorite recipes for wild game, including squirrel stew, roasted wild goose, and quail hash. The book reveals that Ike liked nothing better than catching a fish, building a fire, and grilling his quarry creekside, claiming there was no finer eating than a freshly caught trout.

One Rib Doesn't Necessarily Equal One Vote

Elected as the governor for the state of Georgia in 1954, Marvin Griffin's term was at times marred by allegations of corruption, served with a side order of controversy (for example, he was a staunch segregationist, and pledged to keep Georgia's schools segregated "come hell or high water.") Griffin was one of the last politicos to use large barbecues with free food in an attempt to curry favor from the voters. After being denied another term in the statehouse in 1962, he is said to have spoken the now-famous words, "Some of the people who ate my barbecue didn't vote for me."

Totally Q

Head for the Hills Boys, the Politicians are Coming!
In the early days of North Carolina politics, wannabe politicos developed an effective method of bribing—I mean, communicating—their message to potential voters. It was called the "political caravan" which involved grouping up a bunch of vehicles to travel the state andstopping in small towns and hamlets each day. Political stump speeches and handshaking were followed by a huge barbecue feed, which was usually free to the constituency. Thad Eure, who was the secretary of state in North Carolina for almost 60 years (1936-1989), once said that in their heyday, the caravans would "advertise barbecue so much that whenever the caravan would move down the highways and roads of the state, all the pigs and hogs would see them coming and get out of the way."

Brit Royals Diggin' the Dogs
The 32nd president of these here United States was Franklin D. Roosevelt. On June 11, 1939 he hosted the king and queen of England for a picnic at his estate in Hyde Park, New York. Included on the menu that evening were Nathan's Famous hot dogs cooked on the grill. The printed menu noted that the hot dogs would only be served "weather permitting." Reports say the king enjoyed his "hot dog sandwich" so much that he asked for seconds. Apparently, there was quite an uproar around the country prior to the event, as some super stuffy Americans felt the Roosevelts were somehow acting without dignity by offering their royal guests the lowly tube steak. I guess FDR showed them.

LBJ Knew how to 'Cue
Barbecue *is a noun, a verb, an adjective and in Texas it can be a major social event, as it was whenever President Lyndon B. Johnson called in Walter Jetton to prepare one of his barbecues at the LBJ Ranch on the Pedernales River. Chef Jetton presided over the wood fires in the roasting pits, the charcoal fires in the shallower broiling pits. And the Dutch ovens wherethe beans were simmering, with East Texas hot-guts (a spicy sausage), ready nearby. Accessory foods like steamed ears of corn, potato salad, spicy cole slaw, pickles, sliced onions, and sourdough biscuits were at hand for loading the big tin plates after the basic meats were served by the cooks who sliced them hot and doused them with barbecue sauce. Jetton's formula contains tomato ketchup, cider vinegar, sugar, chile powder, salt, water, chopped celery, bay leaves, garlic, chopped onion, butter, Worcestershire, paprika, and black pepper, all brought to a boil and simmered briefly, then cooled and served.* –Waverly Root and Richard de Rochemont

Lady Bird Shared the Sauce
Things were a little different when Claudia Alta Taylor "Lady Bird" Johnson was the First Lady of the United States from 1963-1969. While in the White House, Mrs.

Totally Q

Johnson would include the recipe for her homemade barbecue sauce when replying to letters she had received.

Kraut for the Kraut, Get it?
During the first ever White House state dinner hosted by President Johnson in December of 1963, Master of Ceremonies Richard "Catus" Pryor (a well-known Texas humorist) apologized to the German delegation because organizers could not find a recipe for barbecued sauerkraut.

The BBQ That Never Was
Probably the most famous barbecue at Johnson's ranch was one that never actually occurred. The date was November 23, 1963 and President John F. Kennedy was being shown around Dallas by then-Vice President Lyndon Johnson, accompanied by a small entourage of politicians and dignitaries. The plan was that after the tour, the parties would board a couple of choppers for the short hop out to Johnson's ranch along the Pedernales River for a barbecue. Unfortunately, a tragic turn of events in downtown Dallas that day canceled the barbecue and remain forever etched in the hearts and minds of all Americans.

Hubert Humphrey Packed Away the Ribs
While cooking at an impromptu victory barbecue at the LBJ Ranch on November 4 1964, legendary Texas pitmaster Walter Jetton served ribs to President Johnson and then- Vice President Hubert Humphrey. Jetton remarked later about the Vice President's eating habits in a cookbook he wrote in 1965. "That guy sure gave these ribs a fit... He went at them like Clyde Beatty to cats and must have eaten them for an hour, putting away more of them than I have ever seen anybody do. So far as I could tell, they did him no harm."

L. B. J. sizing up a steer for one of his epic barbecue parties.

LBJ's Barbecue Diplomacy
Lyndon Johnson probably threw more barbecue parties during his term than any other president. From early on in his political career, Johnson used his ranch in the hill country just west of Austin, Texas to entertain, relax withand lobby his friends, enemies

Totally Q

and fellow politicians. Running mates, diplomats and heads of state all stood before the barbecue altar, which was prepared and tended to by Walter Jetton, the self-proclaimed Barbecue King. Jetton, referred to as a natural showman, was usually dressed in a large Stetson hat, apron, creased white shirt and a bolo tie. Some would say he was the single most influential pitmaster in the history of Texas barbecue. Walter considered himself a barbecue purist: for a pit, he used four large pieces of sheet metal attached at the corners with wire. He built his fire right on the ground (6 inches of sand protected LBJ's lawn) and cooked on a large metal grate. Modern advances such as grills and cookers were thought by Jetton to be nothing but "claptrap."

Johnson used Jetton's barbecue services countless times over the years and even had him cater a rib dinner for supporters on the White House lawn. During the 1964 campaign season, Johnson flew Jetton around the country to work his barbecue magic at numerous political fundraisers as well. After his stint as the country's first ever presidential pitmaster, Jetton published a cookbook titled Walter Jetton's *LBJ Barbecue Cookbook*. The book is out of print today, but is available used on Amazon for around six bucks.

I'll Have Mine Santa Maria Style
President Ronald Reagan (1981-1989) was a huge fan of Santa Maria Style barbecue; in fact, he engaged Bob Herdman and his Los Compadres Barbecue Crew to cater at least five barbecues held on the south lawn of the White House during his presidency. This type of 'cue originated in the Santa Maria Valley, located in the coastal region of central California, during the mid-nineteenth century when area ranchers hosted feasts every spring for their *vaqueros* (cowboys). The featured foods are beef tri-tip, pinquito beans (small pink beans native to the Santa Maria Valley), salsa, tossed salad and grilled bread. Sometimes chorizo or venison is grilled or tossed into the beans, as well.

Presidential Home Delivery
President Jimmy Carter was so fond of the food at Sconyer's Bar-B-Que restaurant of Augusta, Georgia that during his term in office (1977-1981), he had them cater several events for himself and members of Congress on the White House lawn.

Save a Dollar, Barbecue a Congressman
Back in 1981 there was a Congressional dispute about which state had the best barbecue and barbecue sauce. The feud grew from a disagreement between Gene Johnson, a congressman from North Carolina, and John Napier, a representative from South Carolina. To settle the matter, the first-ever Congressional Barbecue Bowl was held on April 1, 1981 , and included entries from many states. I find it very inter-

Totally Q

esting that April Fools' Day was the date chosen for this meaningful event and at first I was quite upset thinking about the mountain of tax dollars that went up in smoke in the interest of good barbecue...not that there's anything wrong with that.

The following year, the event grew as several other members of Congress were pressed into service as judges. Now of course I wasn't there, but I don't think it's fair to speculate that any of the contestants, their special interest groups or lobbyists exerted any undue influence on the judges or contestants. After all, that kind of thing never happens in Washington, D. C. now does it?

Save Room to Eat Those Words

In a weak and belly-stuffed moment back in 1984, Rufus Edmisten, a gubernatorial candidate in North Carolina, made the following statement: "I am through with barbecue." In my mind, this is just like saying "I quit drinking" on the morning after the night before. In his defense, I'm sure he had eaten an awful lot of the stuff as he traveled across the Tar Heel State in search of support. However, this didn't sit well with the Carolina voters as you can imagine—those folks take their 'cue seriously. "You would have thought I had made a speech against my mother, against apple pie, cherry pie, the whole mess," he was heard to say as his team assessed the fallout from his imprudent declaration. I guess it goes without saying, Edmisten lost the election, although it can only be speculated as to whether the barbecue gaffe was actually a contributing factor. It probably didn't help him, that's for sure.

There's a "Truth in Barbecue" Law—I Swear!

In 1986, the South Carolina legislature apparently had way too much time to spare and in its infinite wisdom, crafted and passed what has become known as "The Truth in Barbecue Law." This act required every barbecue establishment within the state to purchase a sticker, (ah, I see, a revenue generator) which had to be displayed prominently inside the window of their joint. The sticker proclaimed to all whether the establishment cooked on wood or used some other type of fuel, and whether they prepared their hogs whole or smoked them in parts.

Now, an examination of the Code of Laws of South Carolina's online database pulled up only one reference containing the word barbecue, and it had nothing to do with restaurants or how they smoked their hogs. It was part of the definitions section, which reads as follows: "...items used or consumed by licensed retail merchants to prepare ready-to-eat food or drink, such as hickory chips, barbecue briquettes, gas, or electricity are subject to tax." Not nearly as interesting as the notion of legislating 'cue, and even though such a law may have been on the books once upon a time, it ain't there now.

Totally Q

Two for the Price of One
First Lady Barbara Bush was known for presenting White House dinner guests with a double-headed recipe card during her time in the White House (1989-1993). On one side she included her family recipe for barbecued chicken. The reverse side contained the formerly top secret recipe for her family's much-sought-after barbecue sauce.

The Bitter Taste of Defeat...and Road Kill
Texas Governor Rick Perry, recent candidate for the Republican presidential nomination, once commented after sampling some barbecued pork shoulder in North Carolina, "I've had road kill that tasted better than that." Although the remark was made back in 1992 during a cook-off between a Texas and a North Carolina restaurant, the statement wasn't forgotten when Mr. Perry decided to dabble in the presidential primary pool. Even though he was surely favoring his home state of Texas, you just have to wonder: What was he thinking? In Being the Consummate Politician 101, don't they teach you never to insult or degrade anyone or anything, unless it is the other candidate or the opposing party? Everyone knows the folks down in Carolina take their pork shoulder seriously and aren't soon to forget a remark like this. My question is this: Has the Guv actually tasted road kill?

Air Force One—Flying Rib Shack?
President Bill Clinton (1993-2001) was giving a speech at Southern Illinois University, and figured because he was in the neighborhood, he would swing by the 17th Street Bar & Grill for a few slabs of Mike Mills' famous ribs—the ones everyone was raving about. Members of the Secret Service advance team had already checked the place out and made the necessary arrangements for the presidential visit and everything was in place for an evening of gastronomical delight.

As the motorcade was heading toward the restaurant, however, the president received a call to return to Washington for some sort of an international incident. These things always seem to pop up at the most inopportune times. While I'm quite sure there were high level discussions held as to whether the incident required an immediate response, a decision was made to reroute the motorcade and head for the airport without making the much-anticipated stop at 17th Street Bar & Grill. I can think of very few requirements that would necessitate canceling a trip to a real-life barbecue Mecca, but I guess that's why I'm not in politics.

It was at this time that someone suggested asking Mike Mills if he delivered. Mike, being the ever-accommodating host that he is, packed up the order and headed toward the airport and Air Force One without skipping a beat or losing a drop of precious sauce. Upon arrival, Mills was invited on board with his packaged goodies and laid out a fine spread of his barbecue delights that is still talked about today. Mike was also treated to an in-person introduction and photo op with the president, making him possibly the only barbecue guy ever to have served a meal to a sitting president on Air Force One.

As Mike was packing his gear and preparing to deplane, he asked one of the Secret Service agents, "How did you know I'm okay to have on board?" The reply he received was: "Don't worry, we've already checked you out. You have top secret security clearance for these few minutes."

Legislating the Hamburger

In 2007, the Wisconsin body politic passed a joint resolution laying claim to the hamburger. Picture both the House and the Senate (a hundred or so people, probably more if you count staffers), sitting around and debating the origins of the hamburger. It's my guess, that this is the only hamburger-related legislation passed anywhere in the United States to this date, but I'm sure it won't be the last. The resolution reads as follows:

The State of Wisconsin
2007 Assembly Joint Resolution

Relating to: Seymour, Wisconsin, as the home of the hamburger,

Whereas, Seymour, Wisconsin, is the right home of the hamburger; and,

Whereas, other accounts of the origination of the hamburger trace back only so far as the 1880s, while Seymour's claim can be traced to 1885; and,

Whereas, Charles Nagreen, also known as Hamburger Charlie, of Seymour, Wisconsin, began calling ground beef patties in a bun "hamburgers" in 1885; and,

Whereas, Hamburger Charlie first sold his world-famous hamburgers at age 15 at the first Seymour Fair in 1885, and later at the Brown and Outagamie county fairs; and,

Whereas, Hamburger Charlie employed as many as eight people at his famous hamburger tent, selling 150 pounds of hamburgers on some days; and,

Whereas, the hamburger has since become an American classic, enjoyed by families and backyard grills alike; now, therefore, be it

Resolved by the assembly, the senate concurring, That the members of the Wisconsin legislature declare Seymour, Wisconsin, the Original Home of the Hamburger. May 9th 2007

Another Barbecue That Never Was

Due to the unforgettable events occurring in our country on September 11, 2001, the Secret Service canceled a planned barbecue on the lawn of the White House.

Totally Q

The following day, the presidential kitchen released 700 pounds of tenderloin beef that had been procured for the gathering and used it to feed some of the hundreds of rescue and first responder personnel who were hard at work in and around the Pentagon area.

Two Slabs to Go, Please

On March 15, 2012, President Obama stopped into Texas Ribs & BBQ in Clinton, Maryland for a quick lunch after giving a speech at a nearby community college. He was accompanied by Maryland Senator Ben Cardin. The POTUS orderd two slabs of baby back ribs for takeout, and unconfirmed reports say he requested extra sauce. President Obama and Senator Cardin chatted with diners and posed for pictures while waiting for their order to be readied. The president even joked that he had to pay up before the order was prepared, although it's my guess that the senator picked up the tab.

Prime Minister Cameron Scores Big

In March of 2012 President Obama presented British Prime Minister Cameron with a Braten 1000 Series Grill, handmade by Engelbrecht Grills and Cookers of Paxton, Illinois. The grill is equipped with a rolling handle that can raise and lower the fire tray to accommodate any style of cooking or heat level, as well as a side firebox for adding a bit of smoke flavor if desired. The president, I am told, even tossed in a pair of personally embroidered chefs' jackets (in case the prime minister and his wife decide to sling some sauce while preparing a rack of ribs for members of parliament). I understand the unit retails for around $1,800, which is a pretty nice gift no matter what side of the pond you are from.

Do You *Pachanga*?

The folks down in south Texas like to call their political parties *pachangas*. Originally, these were events where aspiring politicos could meet with voters in a relaxed setting, usually centered around a barbecue of sorts. As is often the case with simple and successful ideas, however, many of today's *pachangas* have been invaded by corporate sponsorship. Some now include celebrity appearances as well as product giveaways, all done in an attempt to garner voters' support and take their minds off the real issues, which most politicians want to avoid like the plague. Only in America.

The First Lady's Barbecue High Fashion

A 2011 article in *The Guardian* discussed what First Lady Michelle Obama wore to a barbecue where she was not only a guest, but a helper in serving up the grub at 10 Downing Street. Imogen Fox wrote: "In fashion terms the barbecue outfit is a niche sub-genre, which can be very tricky to get right. The look needs to be upbeat and

Totally Q

summery but at the same time involve an outfit able to absorb the odd splodge of tomato ketchup. It's a difficult ask of a dress, especially when you factor in the glare of the world's media looking to dissect the meaning of every last pleat and seam."

As anyone who knows me will tell you, I'm no slave to fashion. I'm the one who is always on the receiving end of a "splodge" of anything sent flying (I'm not even sure splodge is actually a word; if not, it should be). Additionally, I'm not quite sure that any of my sauce-stained shorts or flowered Hawaiian shirts could be described as "upbeat and summery," but they sure are comfortable.

Oh, and just so I don't leave you dying with curiosity, Michelle wore black silk chiffon embellished with crystal. Yep, that would have been my choice too.

Burnt Ends

"...went up to Alexandria to a barbicue."—George Washington, from his diary of 1769

"...a Barbicue of my own giving at Accatinck." —George Washington, from his diary of 1773

"Six miles of roast pig and that in New York City Alone; and roast pig in every other city, town, hamlet, and village in the Union. What association can there be between roast pig and independence?" —Captain Frederick Marryat, reporting on a Fourth of July celebration during a visit to America in the 1830s

"No man should be allowed to be president who does not understand hogs." —President Harry S. Truman (33rd president, 1945-1953)

"Politicians used to believe they could sway votes with a dram of whiskey or a plate of pork. Now they do it with tax cuts and state lotteries. The barbecue was cheaper." —Journalist Jim Auchmutey

"From church to political success, every aspect of life ties back to barbecue." —From the documentary *Barbecue: A Texas Love Story*

"Jesus loved barbecue." —Musician and former Texas gubernatorial candidate Kinky Friedman

 Competition Barbecue

ompetition barbecue has been increasing in popularity ever since such contests first began in the 1970s. Some would argue that 'cue competitions were around before that time, but in the late '80s several early sanctioning groups emerged and started to organize and standardize the events. This helped generate interest from both spectators and contestants alike.

The *Food Network* began regular broadcasts on cable television in 1993, and in my opinion, this was one of the most influential happenings for competition barbecue, as well as all outdoor cooking. The sport had been growing, but the emergence of a 24-hour food channel was like tossing lighter fluid on the fire; things really began to heat up. First broadcast in 2009, *Pitmasters* was instrumental in fueling interest for competition BBQ, especially after the rebroadcast rights were picked up. It is now sometimes possible to watch an entire day of *Pitmaster* shows...and believe it or not, some folks do.

The numbers of both contests and competitors continues to grow, as does attendance for the events. The question remaining in dispute is: *Does competitive cooking qualify as a sport?* If you've read even the most basic definition of the word "sport," I believe you'll agree with me that it is. It certainly fits the definition of sport as "a competitive activity by a group or individual, which is governed by rules, involves physical exertion or skill and can be engaged in professionally." Toss in "an active pastime engaged in for exercise or pleasure," and you've got it nailed—with emphasis on the "for pleasure" part.

Here's another gnarly question to gnaw on: *Is competition barbecue a spectator sport?* Unless you know specifically what you are looking for, being a spectator at a barbecue contest can be pretty boring. Wandering around contest grounds looking at cookers and rigs, surrounded by guys in dirty aprons with funny hats staring at their cookers is not at the top of the average person's list of "things I most want to watch before I die."

Totally Q

In my humble opinion, contest organizers and sanctioning bodies need to do a better job educating the public as to what a barbecue contest is, and what to anticipate when attending one. I've provided a brief overview of what to expect at a KCBS event later in this chapter. As a member of a competition team myself, I've seen many people walking around the grounds with very puzzled looks on their faces; some will even approach and ask what is going on, but most do not. When people who initially were curious about 'cue walk away without a clue about what they've been watching, it's probably the last competition they will ever attend, and that's a shame.

As a group, competition barbecue folks are some of the finest you'll ever meet and are always willing to step up and help others who are new to the game. You want to learn how to cook a decent pork shoulder or rack of ribs? Most of these folks would be glad to give you all the help you need. They are a fun bunch too, which is evident by their crazy team names and banners. If you've never been to a barbecue contest, you need to get yourself out to one this summer—you'll be glad you did. Just do us both a favor and bone up a little before attending. You'll have a lot more fun if you understand what's going on.

The Top BBQ Contests in the United States

Each year, there are literally hundreds of competition barbecue events across the country and millions worldwide. Here are a few of the big dogs:

Cook-Off Craziness

Each year the Kansas City Barbecue Society sanctions more than 400 barbecue competitions throughout the United States, with more than 140 of them taking place during the summer and fall. One of the largest is the American Royal Barbecue Contest in Kansas City in October, where more than 600 judges evaluate the 'cue creations of 400 entrants and ultimately award $30,000 in prizes. This competition and Memphis in May are the foremost championship matches in the world of competitive barbecue.

A Winning Bung Will Get You Jack

Since 1989, during the fourth weekend in October, the town of Lynchburg, Tennessee has rolled out the welcome mat for one of the most coveted invitational contests in the world of competition barbecue, known simply as "The Jack." To even qualify for a chance at an invitation, teams must have won either a sanctioned contest consisting of 50 teams or more, or a contest with at least 25 teams that has been designated as a "State Championship" event.

Totally Q

Those passing muster are then included in the official drawings which take place in every state during early September when each qualifying team's name is placed on a bung and tossed into an oak barrel. Now I know you are wondering what a bung is, and more importantly, what does it have to do with competition barbecue? It's my understanding that *bungs* are defined as stoppers or plugs, sometimes made of rubber or cork, and in this case, are used to close the holes in the oak barrels as part of the fermenting process at the Jack Daniel's distillery. The lucky teams whose bungs are chosen in the drawing then receive one of the much-sought-after invitations; in 2011, 71 teams ultimately competed.

In what has become an annual "Jack" tradition of sorts, a team can purchase a souvenir barrel top that has been embossed with the contest logo. The lucky contestants then ask the pitmasters of all the other teams to sign their barrel top, creating what will surely become a highly cherished memento for years to come.

Think the team from Pig Skin BBQ was happy when they won the 2012 Grand Champion prize at The Jack? Yuuuuup. Photo courtesy Jack Daniel's

American Barbecue Royalty

In 2012, the American Royal Association acquired the rights to the National Barbecue Hall of Fame, with plans create a permanent display and hold yearly inductions during the American Royal World Series of Barbecue, held each October in Kansas City. The Hall already has seven members: Fred Gould, Rich Davis, Speed Herrig, Mike Mills, Carolyn Wells, Gary Wells and John Willingham. The most recent inductees include Johnny Trigg, Guy Fieri and Henry Ford.

Totally Q

I Wonder If They BBQ Bull Balls

In 1974, a barbecue contest was added to the long-running Houston Livestock Show and Rodeo, an event that currently attracts more than 350 barbecue teams each year. Billed as the "World's Championship Bar-B-Que Contest," this competition is used as a kickoff for the livestock and rodeo show, but judging by the ever-increasing numbers of spectators, it would appear that the cook-off is a crowd pleaser in its own right. According to the event's website, 244,184 people attended in 2011, topping 2010's record of 221,229.

All Royaled Up in BBQ Heaven

The first American Royal Barbecue Contest was held in Kansas City, Missouri in 1980. Now known by its trademarked name, the American Royal World Series of

Barbecue©, or "The Royal" for short, this event has exploded from its humble beginnings to become the world's largest barbecue contest. It is held the first weekend in October and attracts more than 60,000 spectators during a four-day run. The site alone is huge, and sometimes referred to by area residents as "Twenty Acres of Barbecue Heaven."

In 2011, the event included more than 500 teams in the Open Contest and 135 teams in the Invitational Contest. The logistics involved for these two contests alone, including organizing, setting up, facilitating and loading the teams in and out are enough to give even the most astute contest planner a huge headache. My head hurts just thinking about it.

According to contest organizers, last year's teams at The Royal rubbed, mopped, smoked and sliced more than 100,000 pounds of barbecued meats. What happens to all that meat, you ask? Here's a testament to the generosity and compassion shown by folks involved in the sport of competition barbecue: According to the official website, in 2011, the barbecue teams, working in conjunction with Harvesters Community Food Network, donated 4,693 pounds of cooked competition barbecue meat. The teams also contributed 987 pounds of additional food drive materials, which added up to 5,680 pounds of provisions for the local food bank to help feed the area's hungry.

Memphis in May: Smell the Smoke

This contest was first held in 1987 on an empty lot north of the Orpheum Theater in Memphis, Tennessee. The following year the event was moved to Tom Lee Park on the banks of the Mississippi River, where it is still held today, providing the area is

Totally Q

not under water (as it was in 2010). In the 1980s, the contest organizers decided to take their format on the road and began sanctioning barbecue cooking contests all over the country. The winners of these events were guaranteed a spot in the World Championship held in Memphis each May, which by then had grown to more than 200 teams.

There's Nothing Like a Good Pork in the Park

Pork in the Park National BBQ Cookoff is the second largest Kansas City Barbecue Society-sanctioned event in the country. It's held each April in the town of Salisbury, located on Maryland's famous Eastern Shore and is considered the season opener for many Northeast teams. From its humble beginnings about 10 years ago when organizers fielded 19 teams, Pork in the Park has grown to hosting as many as 142 teams and now includes a large backyard event held the Sunday after the KCBS contest folks pull out. In the past, spectator attendance numbers have exceeded 35,000 for the three-day event.

What You Can Expect at a KCBS Barbecue Contest

After cooking in numerous barbecue contests over the last six years, I'm continually amazed by the number of folks who approach my site and ask me to explain exactly what is going on. Nothing is worse than having a contest attendee go storming off after I explain to them on Friday night that I don't have any samples of 'cue for them to eat. What follows is a short synopsis to be used as a general guideline for contest goers. Even though it deals with events sanctioned by the Kansas City Barbecue Society (KCBS), the general principles can be applied to most barbecue contests:

The cook teams begin to arrive early on Friday morning. Upon arrival at the contest site, their meats will be inspected by contest reps to ensure that no seasoning or injecting has been done beforehand. Once the meats have been inspected, teams are free to begin any seasoning or injecting for the contest.

On Friday afternoon, teams prep their meats and get ready for the contest cook. During a stroll through the grounds, you will see cookers and smokers of all shapes, sizes and configurations. Friday is a good time to visit with some of the cooks and pitmasters, but make sure they are not involved in contest prep when you ask a question. You will find that most of these folks are more than willing to talk about barbecuing and grilling as long as they are not busy with contest matters.

Many teams will begin cooking their larger contest meats (butts & briskets) late on Friday night or early Saturday morning. If you are on the grounds Saturday morning, you will find the smoke really rolling as teams are busy getting things ready for the most important time of the event, the "turn-ins."

Totally Q

Saturday morning between 11 a.m. and 1:30 p.m., the teams will be extremely busy getting their contest submissions to the judges. This is not a good time to ask questions. Turn-ins are complete after 1:30 p.m. and teams once again will have time to interact with the public.

The turn-in period is probably the best time to be a spectator at a barbecue contest. The teams are working hard to get their succulent selections into their turn-in boxes and make them look just right, as appearance is almost one-third of the overall score. If you take up a position within view of the teams' main prep area, you will be able to see what they go through to get their products ready for the judges' inspection.

The completed entries are then delivered to the judges' tent and must be submitted within a ten-minute window. Many folks wonder who gets to judge all of this barbecue goodness, and the answer is very simple: KCBS-certified judges.

Of course, many folks want to taste the teams' contest offerings. Handing out food samples to the public falls under the jurisdiction of the local county health department, rules and regulations vary from county to county. It's best to check with the contest organizer or look for signage pertaining to sampling when you arrive at the contest grounds.

This is what it's all about: a delectable box of smoked meat ready for judging.

Totally Q

After the last turn-in, teams will begin cooling their cookers and packing for departure. The awards ceremony is usually held around 5 p.m. when the winners of each category, as well as the overall winners, are announced. Teams attend this gathering in hopes of hearing their names called, and all spectators are invited to observe and cheer on the winning contestants. Afterward, some teams will remain on site and this is a good time to visit with the cooks as they sit around and discuss the contest results.

Please remember that the teams involved have made a substantial investment of both time and money to compete in the event. Be respectful when asking questions. Please treat their cooking areas as you would their campsite or even their home kitchen—don't just walk in without permission. Using a bit of common sense and courtesy will go a long way in making your visit to a contest memorable, and one that we hope you will want to repeat time and time again.

If the event you are planning to attend is sanctioned by an organization other than KCBS, it's a good idea to check the group's website prior to attending to be sure you do not miss out on any of the action. For information pertaining to KCBS contest rules or becoming a KCBS certified barbecue judge, you can visit www.kcbs.us/

A Slice of the BBQ Life

Here's a fun peek into the charred, smoky, greasy world of competition barbecue folks. Maybe it will help you understand what drives these crazy pitmasters...or maybe not. I'm one of 'em, and I still haven't figured it out.

Slap Yo Daddy Knocks It Outta the Park

The historic event occurred on July fourth, 2009 at the Way Out West BBQ Championship, held in Stockton, California. Pitmaster Harry Soo from Diamond Bar, California, and his competition barbecue team named Slap Yo Daddy were competing in this KCBS-sanctioned contest and the format called for teams to cook in all four main categories to be eligible for the overall or Grand Championship trophy. The categories were chicken, pork ribs, pork shoulder, and beef brisket; Harry and his team took first place honors in *all four* main categories that year, which of course, made their team the Grand Champion. A feat such as this is very rare in the world of competition barbecue, about as rare as an ice cube in the Sahara Desert.

What Smokes in Vegas, Stays in Vegas

On March 30-31, 2012 in Las Vegas, Nevada, Ron Cates and his Smoke On the Water Productions held what is considered to be the richest barbecue contest to date, with a total prize pool of $50,000 up for grabs. The event was a KCBS-sanctioned cook-off and held in conjunction with the American Country Music Awards ceremony,

Totally Q

which was taking place the same weekend. There were 111 teams competing, and the winner was Harry Soo and the Slap Yo Daddy barbecue team—yup, the same guys who aced the Way Out West Championship in '09—with Lucky's BBQ taking home the reserve Grand Champion honors.

The Murphysboro Legend

Around the barbecue world, Mike Mills of Murphysboro, Illinois is known as "The Legend." Why, you ask? Well, for starters he's the head pitmaster for six widely acclaimed barbecue restaurants, including two located in Las Vegas, Nevada and he's a partner in a New York City barbecue joint by the name of Blue Smoke. Additionally, he was co-captain of the championship team Apple City Barbecue, which has won theWorld Champion award at Memphis in May three times and the Grand Champion award at the Jack Daniel's World Invitational Barbecue Contest in 1992. He is the co-author, along with his daughter Amy Mills, of the very popular book *Peace, Love, and Barbecue*, has won countless awards and in 2010 was inducted into the Barbecue Hall of Fame. Any more questions?

Live, Breathe, Eat BBQ

When asked by Richard Wachtel, host of the *Grillin' with Rich* website, what it is she likes about competition barbecue, Danielle Dimovski (a.k.a. Diva Q) gave this response:

"I love the people and the camaraderie—it is infectious. I also love to win. I love the traveling around and meeting new folks and reconnecting with those I don't see often. I love the thin wisps of smoke in the middle of the night. I love hearing Sully yell "BBQ" at a contest. It makes me smile. I love watching teams try to shig off of one another it cracks me up. I love the BS good-natured smack talk. I love the smell of burning wood charcoal and pellets. I love looking over the competition field and knowing that I am there. I love walking to the stage. I love seeing hard work and practice pay off. I love talking to random folks about why I love BBQ so much. I love seeing a new team get their first call. I love hearing my team name called last. I love the Damn dip. I love when the BBQ Guru guys bring out their very best tequila. I love knowing that if I have had a sucky cook that there are folks that will say a kind word. I love listening to folks talk about their BBQ war stories...I truly live, breathe, eat BBQ."

Maybe They Need to Test the BBQ Judge's I.Q.

Cooks in the KCBS series have been clamoring for years to have the judges include comment cards along with their scores. Several years ago, KCBS, in the interest of harmony amongst the membership and in an attempt to show they were really listening, decided to institute an optional comment card that provides space for brief

Totally Q

judge's remarks which can be either good or bad. Sounds good on paper right? Well, Dan Hixon, pitmaster for the 3 Eyz Championship barbecue team told me about what happened to him a few years ago at a contest in Middletown, Delaware, where he took home the first place trophy in the rib category. After the awards, (keep in mind, he had taken first place), Dan was given a comment card from a judge who gave him scores of 3, 4, and 5 (based on a scale of 2 as the lowest and 9 as the highest potential score). The judge's written comment, however, only served to further

Ever heard that phrase "you are what you eat?" These swine-lovin' ladies are taking it seriously.

confound and flummox Dan when he read, "ribs looked like artificial food."

"Baaaaaaaaaaaaaaabeeeeeeeeeeeequuuuuuuuuuuuuueeeeeeee!"
There's a guy from up New England way who cooks on a competition team named Lunchmeat. His name is Mike Sullivan, but most folks know him as Sully and he's recognized throughout the competition circuit for his boisterous barbecue cheer during the turn-ins and the awards ceremony at many of the contests where his team cooks.

"Baaaaaabeeeeeequuuuuuueeeeeeee!" or some rendition thereof, can be heard from Sully as he walks the contest grounds, while the teams ready their boxes for the judges. Many times, an echo of sorts can be heard from the other competitors, and some of the spectators as well. Back in 2011, while at a contest in New York, someone allegedly complained about the performance, saying it was not keeping within the bounds of acceptable contest behavior. You have got to be kidding. Sully was told to cease and desist until a ruling could be made by the powers that be. "Free Sully" was the cry that emerged from the numerous forums frequented by many barbecue cooks and pitmasters, and the KCBS board of directors convened a meeting to discuss the issue. It was determined that as long as the barbecue cry wasn't sung out during contest quiet hours, it was perfectly legal and acceptable. Who says that common sense is dead?

Totally Q

All the Bad Stuff Up in Smoke

Each year, on Friday night at the Jack Daniel's World Championship Invitational Barbecue contest held in Lynchburg, Tennessee, the organizers hold a dinner for the teams on what has been named Barbecue Hill. Barbecuers and pitmasters attending the event are asked to write down their lists of regrets on sheets of paper, which are then collected and held (in complete confidence, of course) until the appointed hour on Friday evening when they are loaded into the belly of Jasper the Pig. The metal Jasper is then moved into a fireplace where the papers are doused with a splash or two of Tennessee's finest sipping whiskey as an accelerant, then set ablaze to the cheers of the assembled masses. Tradition says that when the regrets are burned, all is right in the world and folks are cleansed, so to speak. Turns out smoke really is good for what ails you.

Those Guys on the 4:20 Team Can *Really* Smoke

On the East Coast, there are a couple of barbecue teams with interesting names: 4:20 Q and 5-0 BBQ. I understand from some very reliable sources that contest organizers go to great pains to place these two teams at opposite ends of the event grounds, for obvious reasons. I've also heard that when the reps realize that both of these teams have signed up to cook in the same contest, they reach out to Bail Bonds BBQ and Munchies Que Team to ask that they please consider entering the event, again, for obvious reasons.

Judges at the Jack Daniel's competition have a difficult task: taste all the entries without busting a gut. Photo by Mike Stines

Totally Q

What's In A Name?

My Favorite Names of Barbecue Cook-Off Teams

Great Boars of Fire
Super Swine Swizzlers
Hazardous Waist
Pork, Sweat & Tears
Seven Basted Bubbas
The Smoke-A-Holics
The Grate Pretenders
Dr. Frank 'n' Swine
Asleep at the Grill
Cayenne Social Club
Swine Flew
Slaughterhouse Five
Aporkalypse Now
The Smokepranos

She Thinks My Slabs are Sexy
Serial Griller
Masterbasters
Dr. Squealgoods BBQ
Pigs, Wings and Other Things
Saucy Butts
Notorious P.I.G.
Ribbed for Your Pleasure
Butt-A-Bing
Albert EinSwine
Swine Done Fine
Smoke in Da Eye

Pig Floyd
Bacon Me Crazy BBQ
The Grill is Gone
R2-BQ
Grill Billies
Too Sauced to Pork
Fat, Drunk & Stupid BBQ
Hot Grill on Grill Action
Church of Swinetology
Slap Yo Daddy
Too Sauced Too Pork
Burnt Reynolds BBQ

My Favorite BBQ Cook-Off Contest Names

Texas Dead Cow Cookin' & Bean Fixin' Extravaganza, Wichita Falls, TX
Big Pig Jig, Vienna, GA
Swine Days, Natchez, MS
Hogtoberfest, Roanoke Rapids, NC
Hog Wild, Jackson, MS
Best Butt in Georgia, Moultrie, GA
Pig in the Park, Winter Park, FL
Meat on the Mississippi Barbecue, Caruthersville, MO
Bubba Fest, Spartanburg, SC
Wurstfest, New Braunfels, TX
Jiggy with the Piggy BBQ Challenge, Kannapolis, NC
Don't be Cruel BBQ Duel, Tupelo, MS
Swine & Dandy Charity Cookoff, Duluth, GA
Brick, Broncs & BBQ, Russell, KS
Big Butts BBQ Festival, Abbeville, SC

Squealin' in the Square, Laurens, SC
PorktoberQue, Dothan, AL
Battle of the Brisket, Mission, KS
Ribs, Rods and Rock and Roll, Vermillion, SD
Stand by Your Grill, Fulton, MS
Pigs & Watermelon Summer Festival, Westminster, CA
Maddison Ribberfest Barbecue and Blues, Madison, IN
Roast and Boast, Columbus, MS
When Pigs Fly BBQ and Fly In, McPherson, KS
I Got Smoked at Westfair, Council Bluffs, IA
Troy Pig Out, Trot, NY
Keepers of the Fire BBQ, Mayetta, KS
Pork in the Park, Salisbury, MD

Totally Q

'Cue For a Cause

When the mesquite, oak, or hickory chips are down, everybody in the barbecue community puts aside the idea of winners and losers and pitches in to help. The following entries show the truest expressions of generosity from the Brotherhood of 'Cue (Sisters included, of course), acts that you'll see over and over again, all across the country.

Cancer Sucks

Scottie Johnson is the pitmaster for a competition barbecue team formed in 2006 named CancerSucksChicago.com, which he started after losing his wife, Corliss, to cancer. He also founded the Corliss Johnson Memorial Foundation that is funded with any and all cash won on the barbecue circuit. To that end, Scottie has won his share of contests, including the 2006 Jack Daniel's World Championship Invitational Barbecue in Lynchburg, Tennessee. Additionally, the Johnson family has pledged that 100 percent of all monies raised by the foundation will go to fight cancer or assist those who are battling the disease.

Operation BBQ Relief

This group sprang up in May of 2011 after a devastating EF-5 tornado tore through the town of Joplin, Missouri, killing 140 people. Pitmasters, along with others in the barbecue world, organized and served more than 12,000 barbecue meals to displaced residents and emergency personnel who were on the scene of the disaster. After seeing how their work helped the folks in Joplin, the core group of volunteers decided to stay together and respond to other events as needed. Their admirable mission statement pretty much sums it up: "The mission of Operation BBQ Relief is to provide compassion and to offer hope and friendship to those whose lives have been affected by natural disasters across the United States through our expertise in cooking and catering barbecue meals and our ability to quickly mobilize our teams into any area where nature disrupts and tears apart the lives of Americans."

A Funny Thing Happened on the Way to the Awards Ceremony...

On June 22-23, 2012, the Second Annual Queen City Barbeque Cook-off was held in Clarksville, Tennessee to benefit the Wounded Warrior Project. Organized by the Queen City Businessmen's Association, teams were given the option of allowing a warrior to assist with contest preparation and cooking during the event. All of the teams agreed, and at the Friday night cooks' meeting, the wounded warriors were introduced to the teams they would be cooking with for the weekend. This idea was a huge success, for the teams as well as the warriors.

During the awards ceremony, something very unusual began to happen. A line

Totally Q

started to form in the stage area near the place where the checks had been given out, because many of the teams had chosen to give their contest winnings back to benefit the Wounded Warrior Project. According to the contest organizers, more than $4,000 of the $6,500 total prize money was returned for the cause. This is incredible, especially considering how much it costs teams just to cook at one of these events. Robert Marion from 2 Worthless Nuts Barbecue Team, who cooked the event and finished third overall, said that when the awards ceremony was over, there wasn't a dry eye in the place.

The Generosity of Midnite Smokers
Husband and wife team Paul and Brenda Hess from Willow Street, Pennsylvania, have been cooking the contest circuit for about ten years with their team, PA Midnite Smokers. Together they have racked up a very respectable list of Grand Championships and other top finishes, including the Grand Champion honors at the New Holland Summer Fest, held each August in New Holland, PA—for an unprecedented four years in a row. Many teams that cook on the East Coast know Paul and Brenda and are very aware of their cooking abilities and their continual threat to capture the top honors, along with the associated cash prize. What most folks probably don't know is that the Hesses donate almost every single dollar they win to charity.

The Shed, With a Little Help From Their Friends
In February of 2012, a large fire tore through the Ocean Springs, Mississippi location of The Shed BBQ and Blues Joint, owned and operated by the Orrison family. In the days that followed, the entire barbecue community turned out to help. Staff, customers, fans, other restaurants, family and friends (most designated as "Shed Heads") showed up on site to assist with clean up and to eventually rebuild. The Shed had been famous for the assorted collectibles and memorabilia displayed around the entire joint and it wasn't long after the flames were extinguished that new stuff began to show up, with folks from around the country sending in all types of great junk to display on the walls of the newly rebuilt restaurant. The Shed was able to begin selling 'cue again a mere five days after the fire, thanks to all of help they received. Today, the folks at The Shed are back to doin' what they do best—serving up some of the finest barbecue and blues in the country.

Totally Q
Burnt Ends

"My drinking team has a BBQ problem!" —Unknown, but I'm sure somebody must have said it.

"The only difference between a 'pro' and a 'backyarder' is the entry fee." —Dan Hixon, Pitmaster of 3 Eyz BBQ Team

"If you want to start your own barbecue team, I suggest finding a couple of folks that share your vision. Believe me when I tell you this: this sounds a lot easier than it is."—Chris Capell, Dizzy Pig Barbecue Company

"In order to be the man, you have to beat the man, and I'm the man." —Myron Mixon of Jacks Old South, Three-Time World Champion

"Barbecue—the only sport where a fat bald man is a GOD."—Unknown

"Barbecue is my golf game, I tell everybody. When you retire, you're supposed to be playing golf. I go cooking." —Johnny Trigg of Smokin' Triggers BBQ Team

"My professional life is on the competitive barbecue circuit and I have no intentions of ever giving up. I want to continue to win because I never want to give up my title of the winningest man in barbecue, and if someone wants to take my throne, they're going to have to work their ass off to snag it from me." —Myron Mixon

"Judges at competitions...usually taste only a bite or two for each entry they are served. If your meat doesn't grab the judges' taste buds and make them whimper with pleasure, the blue ribbon is history." —Chris Lilly

"Competition barbecue...where else would an allegedly sane and clear-thinking person spend large amounts of time and money just to win a six-dollar plastic pig?" —George Hensler, Author of *Startin' the Fire,* the best-selling book on how to start your own barbecue team. Hey, wait a minute, that's me...okay, so I made up the "best-selling" part.

"Being a female, I hate asking anyone for help. For example it's always a challenge backing up my trailer...I mean I will tell them, 'Thanks for being a gentleman, but let me do it.' I refuse to let them do it. I will back it up 50,000 times before I will ask." —Lee Ann Whippen of Wood Chicks BBQ

Meat Market: What's on *Your* Grill?

et's face it: meat is the star of any barbecue, cookout or outdoor gathering, and it has been this way since the dawn of man. While there is nothing wrong with a good salad, a side of slaw, or a creamy potato salad, few things can start the gustatory juices flowing faster than the intoxicating aroma of a couple of rib-eyes over a charcoal fire on a still summer's evening.

In this chapter, I originally set out to cover any and all proteins you might put on the grill or in your smoker and quickly realized I had bitten off a little more than I could chew. While I couldn't hit them all, I think I've covered many of the major players, and touched upon some of the minor or more obscure candidates. I even found a few that might be considered questionable or unusual—such as *cabeza*, or barbecued cow's head—and Rocky Mountain Oysters. Also included is a discussion about an increase in overall breast size over the last 33 years, which I know will be of much interest to our male readers out there. But of course, I'm talking about chicken breasts, so get your mind out of the gutter.

A Nod to Not Dogs
Now don't get me wrong, I'm not suggesting that non-meat eaters be excluded from your backyard activities—that wouldn't be fair. In fact, there are plenty of items available to serve in lieu of meat and I found more than a few vegan barbecue options including "veggie dogs," which are non-meat hot dogs. I'm not claiming that there is a lot of actual meat in a regular hot dog, but I'm just not quite sure I would ever want to devour a grilled "not dog" instead.

I also found that vegans prefer that you clean your grill grates really well before tossing on that tofu burger or veggie dog because they don't want their food touching grease or meat drippings; I guess they prefer their barbecue without taste. It was even suggested on one site that the host provide a completely separate and dedicated grill on which to prepare the non-meat offerings. I think this might be where I would have to draw the line, but that's just me.

Totally Q

Sometimes, Bigger Ain't Better

Texas pitmaster Walter Jetton provided some practical advice to a Minnesota lumberjack who had written him to ask for guidance about cooking a whole steer over a pit. The answer made a lot of sense, particularly for a novice barbecue cook: "First, we would suggest you abandon the idea of a spit, and instead of trying to barbecue the beef in quarters or halves, just buy eight- to 10-pound pieces of boneless brisket points."

Texas Wins With the Most Moos

The total production of cattle and calves in the state of Texas during 2012 was 6.8 billion pounds. This accounted for about one-sixth of the production for the entire United States. Nebraska was second with 4.6 billion pounds, while Kansas contributed 4.1 billion pounds.

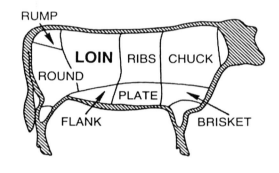

Did that Chicken Cross the Road to Get Onto Your Plate?

Chances are, if you are dining on a plate of barbecued yardbird, your main course came from Georgia, Arkansas, North Carolina, Mississippi, Alabama or Texas. These six states lead the rest in broiler chicken production, an industry that exceeds $1 billion in revenues.

Poultry Breast Augmentation

Scientists tell us that in 1980, about 10 percent of a chicken's total weight was breast meat and in 2007, that figure had risen to 21 percent. In this case, bigger, fuller breasts are not a bad thing. But then, are they ever?

Drexler's Regulars

When turning a rack of spare ribs into Saint Louis style ribs, there's always a bunch of leftover trimmings including the breast bone, back flap and other scraps, which are used by cooks in a number of creative ways. The pitmasters at Drexler's Barbecue in Houston, Texas season up these little nuggets and toss' em on the smoker right along with the ribs, which makes great nibblers for the cooks and their assistants. They call these tidbits "regulars," so if you ever get a chance to stop in at Drexler's, be sure to ask for them by name. You'll be glad you did.

Totally Q

BaaaaaaaBQ

Although a variety of meats are smoked at the Owensboro Bar-B-Q Championship held every May in Kentucky, barbecued mutton comprises the largest share of the one ton of meat that is served up each day of the competition. The locals—descended from Dutch settlers who raised sheep—say mutton is a natural because it needs the long smoking to release its flavor, while younger lamb does not.

Getting Your Goat in Texas

Because of the culinary influence from northern Mexico, particularly the state of Nuevo León, goat has always been a popular barbecue meat in Texas. This is particularly true for *cabrito*, the young, milk-fed goat that is usually slaughtered at the tender (and I do mean tender) age of one month. Perhaps the biggest goat celebration in Texas is the World Championship Barbecue Goat Cook-Off, held every Labor Day since 1974 in Brady. In addition to the meat prepared by competition cooks who come from around the country, the locals also smoke as many as 150 goats to serve to the general public.

Spare Me the Ribbing

Do you have any spare ribs? This question can be taken two ways: If you have some spare ribs, perhaps you'd be willing to share with friends. If you have extra ribs (causing some to be spare) you'd quickly become very popular with folks in the area.

The most frequent use of the above phrase is when you ask your friendly neighborhood butcher for a particular cut of ribs that you're planning to cook, namely spare ribs. A larger cut of ribs than baby back ribs, they are favorites among competition barbecue cooks. These guys will sometimes ask for "Three-and-a-half down ribs," referring to the weight of the rack before cooking. Because this is the most sought-after rib size, it is sometimes hard to find. To make things even more confusing for the amateur barbecuer, a rack of spare ribs can be trimmed and sold as Saint Louis cut ribs, which are much easier to cook and eat than those that are untrimmed.

Pork ribs are a favorite for competition BBQers everywhere. This little piggy was seen at the 2003 American Royal. Photo by Mike Stines.

93

Totally Q

America Goes to the Dogs

During Hot Dog Season, Memorial Day to Labor Day, Americans typically consume seven billion hot dogs, which translates to 818 consumed every second during those months.

Cabeza 'Cue

Down south Texas way, around the Rio Grande area, the locals like to cook up what they refer to as *cabeza*, or as it is more commonly known, barbecued cow's head. At this point you're undoubtedly dying to know how to prepare this delicacy, so I'll tell you. The first thing you need is a 20- to 25-pound cow head. I'm sorry, but I do not have a source or a "guy" for this item. You know, it's always good to have a "guy." I have a computer guy, a car repair guy and a crab guy, but, unfortunately—or fortunately depending on how you look at it—I do not have a cow head guy. You're on your own here.

Anyway, you take the head (I can't believe I am saying this) and skin it, then season it well with salt and pepper. Wrap it in maguey leaves, (nope, no source for those either), and bury the entire package in a hole filled with hot coals. Cover the hole with the excavated soil and leave the pit undisturbed for about 8-10 hours.

I'm told some of the more preferred selections are the eyes, lips, cheek, tongue and ears. Tacos and burritos are sometimes made using the meat from this cooking method, with a 20-25 pound head yielding about 2 pounds of usable meat. One recipe I read advised against cleaning or picking the meat too much, because the mucilage and fat is where much of the flavor originates. All I can say is: *yum.*

These Oysters Have Never Seen the Sea

I was flipping through Ardie Davis and Paul Kirk's book *America's Best BBQ*, when I saw an appetizer called Rocky Mountain Oysters, a.k.a. RMOs, which are reportedly a real crowd pleaser out at Hoke's Genuine Pit BBQ in Westminster, Colorado. As a lifelong resident of the state of Maryland who has enjoyed the bounty of the Chesapeake Bay for many years, this recipe caught my eye. I didn't know they had oysters out West. They must be harvested from lakes or rivers in the Rocky Mountain states, I thought, and until I read the ingredients, I had no idea that they were actually writing about the last part over the fence.

I glanced over at the ingredients list and saw the first item: *5 pounds of frozen bull testicles.* You gotta be kidding. You want me to eat bull balls? In the book, they are described as "rich and good." Now, I'm pretty open-minded when it comes to eating, but I have to draw the line at bull balls. Whether you call them RMOs, Rocky

Totally Q

Mountain Oysters, Pig Fries (hog balls) or chicken nuggets (chicken balls)...all right, I made the last one up...I still ain't eatin' them. I just can't get past the thought, nor do I watch food shows that highlight eating bugs or brains or anything of the sort. If this makes me a food prude, so be it, but I am not eating bull balls.

It's my thinking that ordering up a plate of RMOs is done only to impress a group of friends, sort of a macho thing, as in: *Hey, bring me a platter of those bull balls!"* said with a puffed-out chest and a mug of beer in hand. With that in mind, I also believe that the wait staff rarely receives requests such as: *Excuse me, could you please ask the chef to stop by our table? I simply must have his recipe for these bull balls, they are just divine.*

No Babies Were Harmed in the Making of these Ribs
Baby back ribs, contrary to what some folks think, are not ribs from a baby hog, but instead are cut from the same area as pork loin and pork chops. Sometimes also called loin back ribs, they are a little smaller than spares and tend to cook a bit faster. Most times, baby backs require a lot less trimming than do the spares.

When cooking either cut of rib, be sure to remove the membrane from the bone side of the slab before cooking. Sometimes this membrane will be removed by the packer (especially with baby backs), but typically you will find it intact on spares. If you forget to remove it, don't worry, your guests will remind you soon after their first bite... and you might not like hearing what they have to say.

Barbecued Pig Snoots
The exact opposite of RMOs (the last over the fence), is the snoot, which, as we all know, is the first to make it over. Frankly, I'm a bit skeptical of any recipe that starts off with instructions to boil the meat for over an hour with a cautionary note about the white foam or scum that will develop in the pot. As if that isn't enough, snoot meat is then cooked on the grill for 1-1/2 or 2 hours over indirect heat, and finally gets sauced before serving. The recipe also contains recommendations about what to do when you encounter bristly whiskers. I believe I'll pass.

Totally Q

Zen and the Art of the Perfect Patty

Check out this quote from Elisabeth Rozin: "The meaning of the burger is as a kind of common denominator of the beef experience, with all the flavor, aroma, tenderness, and juiciness in a cheap and accessible form. The meatiness, the beefiness, the succulence of the fat are all there in that unassuming little patty. For perhaps for the first time ever, the hunger for all that beef is, for all that beef represents, can easily be satisfied, is available to almost everyone—and it is perfectly clear that almost everyone wants it. It provides a genuine fulfillment of that atavistic craving in all of us for tender roasted meat running with fat and juice, a hunger that seems to have been a common part of our shared experiences as human beings." Hunger, succulence, craving, fulfillment, juice? It might be just me, but it sounds like Liz needs to have her patty pressed.

Grind Me Kangaroo Fine, Sport

Down on the continent of Australia, you can find kangaroo meat in just about any grocery store and offered in many of the country's restaurants. Here in the States, you will most likely have to buy it frozen. The meat has a beefy flavor, is high in protein, low in fat and when minced or ground, can be used in just about any recipe that calls for ground beef. I also hear that after eating some, you'll jump higher and be a better boxer.

The Hot Dog, Deconstructed

According to the National Hot Dog and Sausage Council, hot dogs are cured and cooked sausages consisting mainly of pork, beef, chicken and turkey, or a combination of meat and poultry. They go on to say that the meat used in hot dogs comes from the muscle of the animal (I guess that rules out the lips and assholes), and looks a lot like the meat products you might find in your grocer's meat case. I'm not quite sure I really believe that last statement, but if that's their story, I guess I'll go along.

Other ingredients include water, curing agents and assorted spices. The Council goes on to state that if "variety meats" are used, the manufacturer must specify which ones are included. They say livers and hearts are considered "variety meats," but they make no mention of feet, feathers, or other assorted possibilities. I won't even mention what turns up on the list when I Google the term.

Different Breeds of Dog (From the National Hot Dog & Sausage Council)

From restaurants and street carts to ballparks and backyard barbecues, hot dogs are everywhere! But depending on where you are, your toppings may differ radically. Here's a short guide on what to expect when you buy your hot dog away from home.
New York City: New Yorkers eat more hot dogs than any other group in the country. From downtown Manhattan to Coney Island, when you buy your hot dog in

the Big Apple, it will come served with steamed onions and a pale, deli-style yellow mustard.

Chicago: The possible antithesis to New York dogs, Chicago dogs are layered with yellow mustard, dark green relish, chopped raw onion and tomato slices, then topped with a dash of celery salt and served in a poppy seed bun.

Atlanta and the South: Buying a hot dog at Turner Field (home of the Atlanta Braves) or elsewhere in Atlanta and the South, you'll end up with your dog "dragged through the garden" —in other words, topped with coleslaw.

Kansas City: Get the mints out—you'll need them when you order up a hot dog in KC, which is served with sauerkraut and melted Swiss cheese on a sesame seed bun.

Baseball Stadiums: Turner Field isn't the only place to get a hot dog styled to local preferences. Here are some others to check out:

The Rockie Dog: Served at Coors Field, the home of the Colorado Rockies, this is a foot-long dog with grilled peppers, kraut and onions.

The Fenway Frank: It's the only dog to eat while watching the Red Sox. It comes boiled and grilled and served in a New England-style bun with mustard and relish.

The Texas Dog: Chili, cheese and jalapeños make this the favored item at Minute Maid Park in Houston. I suppose you could order a side of orange juice too.

Those Are Pretty Good Odds...
According to the 2009 U.S. Cattle Census, there were 9.2 million cows (females) in the United States, and only 2.1 million bulls (males). Reminds me of that joke about the old bull and the young bull standing on top of a hill looking out over a herd of cows. "Let's run down there and have our way with some of those cows," said the youngster. The older and wiser bull looked around and replied, "Why don't we walk down there and have our way with all of them?"

Ostrich is Popular Somewhere
Grilled ostrich is still considered a novelty here in America, but in Australia and Africa this meat is not only accepted, it's very popular. I wonder if they serve fried Ostrich Oysters.

Burnt Ends, You Say?
Folks say burnt ends originally were the scraps and ends created when pitmasters sliced their briskets and some restaurants used to give them away for free. To make your own burnt ends, cube up the point cut, discarding any extremely fatty pieces, then toss the hunks into a pan. Pour in some of your favorite barbecue sauce and some of the separated drippings from your brisket, then return the pan to the smoker. Give the chunks a stir every now and then until they are nice and tender and the sauce adheres to them.

"You know, I wouldn't mind getting my hands on your tenderloin one of these days."

The Most Popular Cuts of Beef

Chasing That Skirt Steak
This is a narrow steak, usually only a few inches wide and less than one inch thick with a grain that runs across its very short width. This cut is often sliced thinly for fajitas or steak sandwiches.

The Tri-Tip
Sometimes known as a culotte steak or triangle steak, this cut comes from a triangle-shaped muscle taken from the end of the top sirloin and weighs, on average, one-half to two-and-a-half pounds. It is very popular on the West Coast, particularly in Southern California (where some say it originated) and has become a favorite with cooks on the competition chili circuit as an affordable prime cut with beefy flavor and low fat content.

New York Strip Steak
Also known as the club steak, shell steak, or Kansas City strip, this cut comes from the loin area which is considered one of the more tender parts of the animal and is certainly among the most flavorful. This cut is often preferred for the dry-aging process used by many of the top-end steakhouses. Considered by some steak aficionados to be the most superior of beef cuts, it's best when served in slices 1-1/2 to 2 inches thick.

Prime Rib
This is the bone-in rib steak taken from ribs six through 12 of the animal. At times, this cut can have some gristle or fat, but it also can be very full-flavored.

Totally Q

Delmonico
A boneless steak taken from the rib section and named after a popular 19th-century New York City restaurant.

London Broil
A larger cut of meat from the flank, London broil has a tendency to be tough unless properly prepared. It's best when grilled quickly and served in very thin slices that have been cut across the grain.

Chateaubriand
The pointed end of the short loin, this cut is usually sized for two servings. When properly prepared, it can be one of the most tender and flavorful cuts around.

Flat Iron Steak
Taken from the chuck portion (the front shoulder or top blade of the animal) and sometimes varying in size, the flat iron is absolutely delicious when properly cooked. What this steak lacks in tenderness, it makes up for in flavor. It's considerably less expensive than other cuts and often has significant marbling, which is always a good thing.

Porterhouse
Considered by many to be the king of steaks or big brother of the T-bone, the porterhouse is made up of both the tenderloin and the New York strip. Best if cut at least 1-¼ inches thick, but many prefer these babies lobbed off in 2-inch-plus slices.

Flank Steak
Taken from underneath the steer's rib area, this is a very dense steak with little or no marbling and is the only one cooked as an entire muscle without being cut to size. Often used to make fajitas, flank steak is best when served rare or medium rare as it can become tough and dry if overcooked.

T-Bone
Taken from the same area as the porterhouse, this cut is named for the shape of its

bone. The porterhouse gets more of the tenderloin than this one, but the T-bone can eat just as good. Like a porterhouse, it's better if served in larger hunks.

Filet Mignon

The French word *mignon* means "dainty or cute," but you shouldn't hold that fact against this filet. Known to some as the "queen of steaks," (don't hold this against it either), this most tender of all steak cuts comes from the smaller end of the beef tenderloin that runs alongside the animal's spine. Filet mignon is always cooked and served boneless and has the distinction of being the most expensive cut. Feel free to hold that against it.

RibEye

This cut is the most heavily marbled of the steaks and therefore is considered the most flavorful. It is taken from the rib section, the same area as prime rib and the standing rib roast, and is the top choice for many steak aficionados. Rib-eye can be served both on the bone or boneless and is best when slices are thicker than 1-1/2 inches

Hanger Steak

This is another one of those cuts that used to be considered junk or tossed into the grind pile, but is now one of the latest "hot licks" in the world of outdoor grilling. The hanger steak, sometimes called the hanging tenderloin, is a long, thin cut from the underbelly of the steer, taken from the area between the ribs and the loin. The muscle, which is not connected to any bone, is located near the kidney (giving it a rich, beefy flavor), and " hangs " from the diaphragm. There is only one hanger steak per animal and the cut, which weighs between a pound and a pound-and-a-half, consists of two long strips of muscle separated by a tough vein that is usually removed by the meat cutter. Because this meat is considered fibrous, it should be cooked quickly, then thinly sliced across the grain for serving.

Sirloin Steak

This cut comes from the rear portion of the animal between the rump or round steak and the short loin. Though it is a less tender cut than some prime beef, a good sirloin steak can be packed with flavor.

What Is a Brisket?

Many folks consider the brisket to be the only real barbecue meat, especially our friends from Texas, and it is also commonly used to make corned beef and pastrami. A beef brisket consists of two parts and can weigh between eight and 16 pounds. It comes from the lower chest of the steer and is part of the muscle structure that supports roughly 60 percent of the animal's total body weight. As a result, it contains

Totally Q

a significant amount of connective tissue which means the meat is extremely tough unless properly cooked. The largest section is called the "flat" or "first cut" and is the most lean of the three. This is what you find marketed as brisket in most grocery stores. The "point", "second cut" or "deckle" is much fattier than the flat and is considered to be more flavorful. Many pitmasters use this piece for making burnt ends.

How Beef Makes the Grade
The United States Department of Agriculture (USDA) is responsible for grading the beef that we eat. For purposes of this discussion, we will concentrate on the three most popular grades of beef sold in most stores around the country.

Select: This is the lowest grade of beef available in most retail outlets. The grade generally has less marbling which means it has less flavor and is tougher to eat.

Choice: The middle of the road, this grade contains some marbling, which translates into decent taste, and more tenderness, if you're lucky. It is the most popular in grocery stores, usually priced below prime and is preferred by meat lovers all across the USA.

Prime: This is considered the highest grade of beef, with the most flavor and taste. It tends to have the best marbling and is usually cut from younger animals. If you want Prime cuts, you typically have to special order them or go to higher end meat distributors.

Certified Angus Beef
The Certified Angus Beef (CAB) program was launched in 1978 by a group of Ohio cattlemen and Angus supporters in an attempt to make quality beef products available to all consumers. Today, "Certified Angus Beef" is a registered trademark owned by the American Angus Association, which boasts more than 30,000 members and the CAB brand sells more than 2.2 million pounds of beef daily throughout the world. According to the group's website, their meat is a notch above USDA prime, choice, or select and must pass ten additional quality standard requirements before receiving the CAB designation.

See the Light and Eat the Dark
It has been beaten into the collective American psyche these past twenty years or so that we need to be eating skinless, boneless chicken breasts anytime we decide to indulge in a meal of yardbird. This type of chicken, we are told, is healthier for us. The fact of the matter is, when it comes to the grill or smoker, most folks—and this is a worldwide opinion—prefer dark meat (legs or thighs) to breasts. The dark pieces contain more fat, which translates to moister, more flavorful meat.

Taking your Steak's Temperature
Unless you have grilled large numbers of steaks and have become proficient in

Totally Q

judging the look of a cooked steak as it relates to the internal temperature, you will need a good thermometer. I would suggest an instant read, digital model. They cost a bit more, but are so much more accurate and reliable than the cheaper spring dial type, that they're definitely worth the investment.

Ideal Internal Meat Temperatures
(in degrees F):

Beef
Rare- 120
Medium rare- 130
Medium- 140
Well done- 160

Pork
Roasts, chops, loins- 145
Ground pork- 165

Chicken
Breast-165
Thighs/legs- 165

I Like Big Butts

The cut known to barbecuers as the pork butt or Boston butt is actually not from the ham, rear, or butt portion of the hog. The term *butt* refers to the top section of the hog's front shoulder. A whole pork shoulder is made up of two parts—the butt portion, which is located on the upper end of the shoulder, and the picnic cut, which is located on the lower front shoulder. In most of today's grocery stores, the shoulder is sold in two separate portions—butt and picnic. Whole shoulders are still available, but usually they have to be special ordered. Both shoulder portions contain a good deal of fat, which makes these pieces excellent choices for barbecue.

Hey Kobe, Do You Wagyu?

Wagyu beef was first introduced to the United States in 1976 and some say the cattle originated from Kobe, Japan, a coastal city known for its excellent beef. The term *wagyu* refers to several breeds of specially-bred cattle, and the meat they produce is reported to have more marbling, and therefore more flavor. Many high-end steak houses use this beef in their menu offerings, and it's available in some grocery stores. While some say the meat is extremely flavorful and tender, others claim it's not much different than Certified Angus. If you want to try it for yourself, be prepared...because wagyu costs more—way more.

What's a Pit Beef Sandwich?

Once known as a strictly Baltimore phenomenon, pit beef sandwiches have spread their wings and are now available in many other locations, particularly on the East Coast. The sandwich is made by grilling top round of beef seasoned with salt and pepper over a hot charcoal fire. The meat is then sliced to order: rare, medium or well, then served on sandwich bread or a roll with horseradish, sliced onions and/or your favorite barbecue sauce. In the Maryland area, these sandwiches are usually sold from roadside stands and are popular as fundraisers for the local American Legion or other civic associations.

Totally Q

The Perfect Burger

Paul Newman co-owned a restaurant in Westport, Connecticut with a chef named Michael Nischan, and the pair set out on a quest to determine what it would take to develop the best tasting hamburger on the planet. After months of work, they came up with the following guidelines. Of course these are not written in stone, but you get the idea.

- Use grass-fed beef; it has a much better flavor.

- For your grinds, use 45 percent brisket and 55 percent chuck.

- Add 22 percent of good beef fat.

- Grind your blend twice. You will get better results if you freeze your grinder before completing this step, although, I will concede this is a little difficult if you are asking your butcher to do the grinding.

- Make your patty about one inch thick and one inch wider than the roll you are using. The finished burger should weigh in at around nine ounces.

- When forming the patty, work fast, without packing the meat too tightly.

- Make a slight depression into the center of the burger when complete. (This helps maintain a consistent size after cooking)

- If you are doing multiple patties, do not stack one on top of another, as this crushes the ones on the lower level.

- Salt the tops and bottoms with a quality sea salt just before cooking.

- Grill over hardwood charcoal.

- Use a spatula for turning and never press down on the top of the burger.

- Do not overcook.

- If adding cheese, do so about two minutes before they are done.

- Let the patties rest for two minutes or so before serving.

- Add about one teaspoon of butter to the top of the burger while it rests.

- Use a good quality roll that you butter and toast lightly over the grill before adding the burger.

- Buy the freshest ingredients possible for garnish.

Burnt Ends

"When a Southwesterner talks about food, he's talking about meat, and he's probably talking about beef." — *A Taste of Texas Cookbook* by Jane Trahey, 1949

"There is simply no other food that inspires more passion among foodies than ribs. People just love to eat ribs, cook ribs, and even just talk about ribs." — Ray Lampe, a.k.a. Dr. BBQ

"Grilled chicken ranks among the world's most popular barbecue. The diversity of its preparation is limited only by the imagination of the world's grill jockeys." - Steven Raichlen

"I'll gladly pay you Tuesday for a hamburger today." —J. Wellington Whimpy, from the Popeye Cartoons

"I think every animal has a right be to barbecued!"—Al Lawson

"Life expectancy would grow by leaps and bounds if green vegetables smelled as good as bacon." —Doug Larson

"All normal people love meat. If I went to a barbecue and there was no meat, I would say 'Yo Goober! Where's the meat!?' I'm trying to impress people here, Lisa. You don't win friends with salad." —Homer Simpson, from the television show *The Simpsons*

"Laws are like sausages. It's better not to see how they are made." —Otto Von Bismarck (1815-1898)

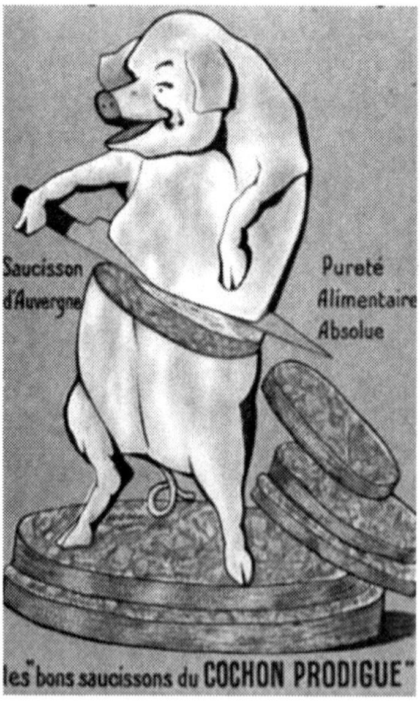

Saucisson d'Auvergne

Pureté Alimentaire Absolue

les bons saucissons du **COCHON PRODIGUE**

Talkin' About Tips, Sauces & Sides

Grilling tips are like opinions (or the lower body orifice sometimes referred to in this old saying)...everybody has one. If you don't believe me, try this little experiment. Take up a position within earshot of the grill at the next barbecue you attend. Post yourself there with a cooler full of cold drinks, so you won't be drawn away unnecessarily and get there early—you won't want to miss a single minute.

What you will notice, as you listen in on the gathering of this bull- and testosterone-fest, is the overabundance of suggestions and the plethora of tips offered to the attending grill master. Some of these might include: "You need a higher flame"; "You're cooking too hot"; "That one needs to be flipped"; and "You should see the grill I just bought!"

When it comes to cooking in the great outdoors, every guy is an expert in his own mind. Of course, somewhere in this sea of unsolicited suggestions there is undoubtedly something that could be considered useful or helpful. The easiest way to determine the worthiness or usefulness of these "helpful" recommendations is to consider the source. Ask yourself the following questions: *Does this guy know what he's talking about? What are his credentials?* Armed with a few snappy and well-placed follow-up questions, you can quickly determine whether the person offering the tip is knowledgeable or just full of bull pucky.

In this chapter, I've collected some tips I thought you *might* find useful. Just remember: you are the master of your own pit and can take any of these suggestions with a grain of salt or a drop of sauce. You're the boss. Grilling tips are like a**holes...everybody has one.

Red Caldwell's Five Ironclad Rules of Barbecue
1. Never salt meat prior to cooking. Salt dries and toughens the meat. This includes

Totally Q

garlic salt, onion salt, seasoned salt, etc.

2. Never use a fork to handle cooking meat. Pierced meat loses juices which causes toughness and dryness. Use tongs or a scoop.

3. Always cook meat fat side up. Let gravity naturally baste and tenderize the meat.

4. Never use a sweet and/or tomato basting sauce until the last 30 minutes of cooking. The sugar caramelizes and burns quickly. Yuck!

5. Always preheat the pit and form a bed of coals. This saves a lot of misery later.

Doctor, Doctor, Give Me the News

Rib Doctor Guy Simpson says that backyard barbecuers often don't have the opportunity to learn the tricks of the trade that competitive barbecuers use all the time. Here, he shares a few tips that will help you turn out mouth-watering ribs every time you cook.

To skin baby back ribs, turn them over and find the second bone in from the end. At this spot, use a Phillips head screwdriver to make a hole in the rib big enough to put your finger through, then pull the membrane off the back of the ribs. This will allow the meat to get smoke from both sides.

Because of all the preparation, barbecuing can be a lot of trouble for just one dinner, so Simpson additionally suggests rolling several racks of ribs into a tube shape, fastening them with string and standing them on end in the smoker. By doing this, you can prepare many ribs at one time and the extras will freeze beautifully for later use, says Simpson, but remember to cut them apart before freezing.

Room Temperature Raw Meat? No Way!

Some folks say you should leave your steaks on the counter and allow them to come to room temperature before grilling them. Steven Raichlen, professor at Barbecue University and author of several great books on grilling, smoking and outdoor cooking, says: NO! Your steaks should be kept on ice or in the refrigerator up until the moment they are tossed on the grill to prevent bacteria growth.

Totally Q

Herb- and Garlic-Flavored Smoke
In addition to the seasoning provided by aromatic hardwoods, various other flavor enhancers can be placed in the firebox near the coals. Whole heads of garlic, especially elephant garlic, produce great results, as do fresh herbs, which are preferred over rehydrated dried herbs. Try using bundles of thyme, basil, Mexican oregano, and cilantro tied together and take care that the herbs do not burn up immediately, but instead generate a nice, slow smoke.

Preventing Those Embarrassing Flare-Ups
Flare-ups occur when dripping fat ignites on the heat source and causes flames to envelop the meat and char it which ruins its flavor, aroma, texture, and color. This situation is easy to avoid if you do the following:
• Pay close attention to your fire and to your cooking. Don't wander away from the grill to watch the game in the living room.
• Make sure the fire isn't too hot. Adjust the heat by turning down the gas or raising the grill above the coals.
• Move dripping meat away from the hottest coals.
• Remove the meat immediately if a flare-up begins. You usually have some warning.
• Keep a spray water bottle handy to wet the coals or douse flaring meat.

Great BBQ? Nothing To It...
Keith Allen of Allen & Son Barbecue in Chapel Hill, North Carolina says cooking good 'cue is easy peasy. "The secret to great barbecue? That's easy. Wake up at 3 a.m. Split and haul a quarter ton of hickory logs each morning and burn them in a pit you built yourself. Roast the pork shoulders over the embers—not burning wood, mind you, embers—for four to five hours per side. Chop the pork shoulders by hand with a meat cleaver and douse them with vinegar sauce. That's all there is to it."

The Ten Commandments of Barbecue, by Rich Davis and Shifra Stein
1. Smoke it slow and keep the fire low.
2. Use high heat only when grilling or searing.
3. Don't trim the fat off brisket and ribs before smoking.
4. Remember that traditionally barbecued meats are well done.
5. Don't confuse grilling with barbecuing.
6. Consider the wind and the outdoor temperature.
7. Learn when to use sauces.
8. Make the best use of wood.
9. Use charcoal briquettes properly.

Totally Q

10. Bring meat to room temperature before cooking.

The Expert Pitman Protests

Luscious "The King" Newsome has some strong opinions about boiling ribs before barbecuing them: "Yeah, you can boil them. Let me tell you, if you do, also buy a pack of noodles. Then when you take the meat out, throw the noodles in so you'll at least have some noodles to eat, because you just cooked the best part off the meat."

Wood is Good

Texas pitmaster Louis Charles Henley was asked for his opinion on the use of wood as a fuel to cook barbecue. He replied, "Wood is the only seasoning I need. I use post oak for the heat, and then I add a little pecan for the sweetness and mesquite for the tang. Your wood has to be well seasoned, at least a year old. Green pecan will make you sick. I never use charcoal—charcoal gives people indigestion. Good wood is the only secret of good barbecue."

Smoke From a Bottle?

Liquid smoke is available in just about every grocery store across the country. Most alleged barbecue purists publicly poo-poo the product, often using it as the brunt of jokes or as fodder for insults hurled at other pitmasters. The fact remains, however, that the product is here, and I'll bet you most of those poo-pooers have a bottle of the stuff in their pantry or cook box. You will also find this ingredient used in many commercially-available barbecue sauces. Debate continues as to whether there are any health risks associated with its use; depending on which way the wind is blowing for the day, it is bad for you or it won't hurt you—you can decide. Liquid smoke is made by condensing and cooling real wood smoke and then collecting the resulting residue. Some say it's about as natural as an unnatural product can get. It has a very strong and distinct taste, so if you are using this flavoring, my advice would be to add it slowly and taste before adding more. You've been warned.

Shish-ka-bob or Shish-ka-bib-bill?

"Anyway, one good thing to make is shish-ka-bobs, which are metal sticks loaded with vegetables and meat cooking unevenly, so you flip them, at which point everything falls into the fire. Or you can use wooden sticks soaked in water, which will hold the meat better, right until they dry out in spite of your considerable efforts and break in two. So it's really up to you how you choose to waste time and money." —From Cracked.com, *How to BBQ Like a Real Man*

Make My Wiener Well Done

"Bold is the man who grills nude before spattering chicken. Bold, and quite possibly drunk. This activity is great fun, so long as your guests are neither dressed nor

Totally Q

mortified. If he survives, he will likely receive a beneficent entendre from a female requesting a hot dog but indicating she already has a bun." —From *The Man's Book of BBQ* by Brendan McGinley

Sound Suds Advice
"A real man drinks beer at a BBQ. You may be tempted by the champagne cocktails going around, but you must resist. Head straight for the beers and don't forget to have your own stubby holder on hand. Remember to never be without a beer in your hand throughout the duration of the BBQ. As BBQ host you must always offer beer to those other real men that are without a beer or running low." —From TheBBQList.com

You Poke It, You Broke It
Harley Goerlitz is known as "The Winningest Barbecuer in Texas," so when he speaks, folks tend to listen, sort of like the E.F. Hutton of the barbecue world. When asked for some words of wisdom for the legions of backyard cookers and smokers, Harley said, "What separates the good from the great is the little things." For instance, he says never use a fork to move or turn your barbecued or grilled meats, always use tongs or a fire glove. Precious juices run out of the holes made by a fork, which causes meat to dry out.

If You're Looking, You're Not Cooking
Jim Goode says a good guideline for cooking brisket is to allow one hour for each pound of meat, cooking at a temperature of 250 degrees F. He also recommends adding 15-20 minutes to your total time every time you open the lid on the cooker. Remember, if you're looking, you're not cooking. Also keep in mind that the average yield for an untrimmed brisket is about half, so a 12-pound cut should give you around six to seven pounds of finished product.

Steak It Like a Man
President Dwight Eisenhower was an accomplished grill master. Popularly known as "Ike," one of his favorite things to cook for guests was New York strip steaks, three inches thick. Although his grilling method was thought by some to be a bit primitive or "out there," word is, once you tasted a steak he had

President Eisenhower flips some steaks with his assistant, Moaney.

109

Totally Q

prepared, all previous thoughts of the president going berserk quickly vanished. First, Ike would make his fire and allow the coals to get white hot, then he coated all sides of the steak (including the edges) with a generous portion of salt and pepper. Now for the unusual part: Using a pair of tongs, he would lay the steak directly onto the coals, turning it after about seven to nine minutes, then allowed five to six minutes on the other side, depending upon the heat level. After removing the steak from the fire, he would lay it on a board and use a wire brush to remove all the ash and salt, then transfer it to a clean cutting board and slice the meat against the grain into ¾-inch pieces. Give it a shot—would a president ever mislead the public?

Keeping 'Cue?
Barbecue will keep for a long time if properly stored. Always be sure to cool your 'cue after serving, but do not allow it to languish at room temperature on a table during a hot spell in August. Refrigeration in a sealed container will work well for a week or so; any longer than that, you'll want to move it to the freezer. The best way to freeze barbecue is with a vacuum sealer, and be sure to date your package. The bag of sealed frozen meat can be re-heated in boiling water or thawed in the fridge, then dumped into a pot and warmed on the stove top. If needed, you can add a little liquid when heating. I like to use apple juice, beer, barbecue sauce or just plain water.

Championship Smoked Ribs
This cooking procedure resulted in a first place rib entry at the 1992 Memphis in May competition for the Apple City BBQ Team of Murphysboro, Tennessee.

Preliminary: The ribs are rubbed with a secret combination of sixteen spices.

Hour 1: The ribs are smoked at a temperature of 100 degrees F.

Hour 2: The temperature of the smoke increases to between 180 and 200 degrees F. and the ribs are basted twice with fresh apple juice.

Hour 3: The temperature increases to 250 degrees F. and the ribs are basted two more times with apple juice.

Hour 4: Two light coatings of a secret finishing sauce are applied and then more of the spice rub is sprinkled over all. Smoke at 250 degrees F. for 30 more minutes, making the total smoking time 3-½ hours.

The Experts Rub it In
"Figure that two cups of rub will yield enough to flavor a couple of briskets or a half-dozen slabs of ribs." —Cheryl and Bill Jamison

"Less than a tablespoon will flavor a whole chicken breast, or dust a 6- to 8-ounce fillet of fish. A quarter cup will easily cover a side of spare ribs, or a whole breast of turkey." —Jim Tarrantino

Totally Q

Tong That Dog
When grilling your hot dogs, most experts agree that you should turn them with tongs rather than a fork. When pierced by a fork, the dogs lose their juice, which reduces overall flavor. Remember, juice is good.

Use a Light Touch with Fish
"BBQ Queen" Karen Adler shares some of her fishy secrets: "Fish and seafood pick up marinade flavors quickly. Marinating for 15 minutes to an hour should be sufficient. Do not over-marinate, or fish flesh will break down and become mushy. At their simplest, marinades and bastes can be a light application of oil with salt and pepper seasoning. Woods and herbs added to the grill offer another means of flavor enhancement. Fish cooks so quickly over a hot fire that your addition of soaked wood chips or herbs will not penetrate as effectively as will slow smoking with a closed-lid grill. But the heavenly odor in your backyard is worth a try."

Give it a Rest!
Most meat, especially steak, eats and tastes better when allowed to rest for a few minutes on a warm platter after being removed from the grill. The theory is that the meat relaxes and is therefore juicier when served. It is also the practice at many steakhouses to top steaks with a tab of melted butter just before serving. Many cookbooks offer recipes for flavored butters that can be used in this way with great results.

Meat on a Stick
The idea of threading hunks of meat onto a stick and hanging it over the fire has been around since the caveman days. Most modern-day recipes advise us to soak the skewers beforehand, which is good advice, especially if they are made of wood, but there are also several cooking methods to help prevent them from catching fire. In some places, for instance, special long, narrow grills are used to keep skewer ends away from the direct heat, but if you are cooking kabobs on a home grill, you can make a guard out of aluminum to place under the tips of the sticks. Yet another idea is to use a hibachi or other type of small tabletop grill because the skewers are longer than the unit, which means the ends will be far enough from the embers to avoid catching fire. If you are feeling really adventurous and your guests have not had too much wine to drink, you can even let each person grill his or her own kabob over the tabletop heat source.

Listen to the Pit
"You don't need a laundry list telling you what to do, just sit on the stump and listen. The chickens will whisper to you when they need to be flipped. The pork will sing

Totally Q

when it is finished cooking. The fire will wink at you when another log is needed. No list, no clock, no thermometer can tell you how to cook barbecue. You just sit in the corner and you just know." This is what World Champion Pitmaster Chris Lilly was told

his first day on the job as an apprentice in the pit room at Big Bob Gibson's Bar-B-Q in Decatur, Alabama. Chris was given this sage advice after watching his mentor toss his notebook containing the day's notes he had diligently taken right into the flames. He must have taken the advice to heart, because if you ask Chris today, he'll tell you he is still sitting on that stump, listening to the pit.

Roll Me a Fatty

Sometime in the not-too-distant past, a quick-thinking barbecue pitmaster was looking for something to nibble on while tending his pit during a twelve-hour brisket cook. He had a roll of Jimmy Dean sausage left over from breakfast

Chris Lilly, a.k.a. The Pit Whisperer.

and thought: *What the hey, sausage is made of pork...why not?* Barbecue historians tell us

he rolled the sausage in his dry rub and threw it on the cooker. When it was done, he brushed on a coating of barbecue sauce, and a new taste sensation was born.

Since that fateful day, the "Fatty" (as it has come to be known) has been taken to amazing levels. Folks roll out the sausage, then stuff the center with all types of goodies—cream cheese, salsa, mushrooms, chopped bacon, brie, pulled pork, green peppers and onions, crab meat, hummus,—just about anything and everything has been used (okay, I made up the part about hummus, but you get the point). Once stuffed, the flattened sausage is then rolled up, sealed on the ends, rubbed, and dropped into the smoke.

There's even a Fatty version known as "the bacon explosion," however, please do not—I repeat DO NOT—Google this term. These days, any excessive Internet inquiries containing verbiage of this type could result in receiving an unwanted visit from a representative of Homeland Security. Therefore, I will tell you how this delicacy is created: Take a Fatty and wrap it completely with a pound or two of bacon before cooking. That's it. Some people even use an interlacing configuration when placing the bacon, which means there's finally an application for those basket weaving skills you learned in school.

The Other Side of Sauces

Each year Americans spend over $350 million on bottled barbecue sauce. If you're among those culinary adventurers who prefer to make their own sauce, here are some tips for you.

Make Great BBQ Sauce
Brother Mel Johnson has a few suggestions for creating your own signature sauce:
• Start with a commercial sauce and doctor it up with chile peppers or other ingredients that you like.
• If you are intent on creating your own, begin with the best grade ketchup you can buy.
• Slow cook the sauce at a low temperature.
• Use a mixture of spices that you like.
• Make a sauce that has a good balance of sweet and hot. That way, it will please almost everyone.

Everybody Liked Ike's Barbecue Sauce
President Dwight D. Eisenhower loved to barbecue, and he once shared his recipe for barbecue sauce with a group of Young Republicans in Connecticut who were holding a rally. They had to make a few adjustments for quantities, because the amounts were scaled for 5 pounds of chicken and they were expecting 1,200 people at the rally—one of whom was Senator Prescott Bush, the father of George Herbert Walker Bush. What follows is the recipe used that day and later included in a great old book titled *Ike, the Cook*. Be advised, however, that this is for the smaller batch that calls for only 5 pounds of yardbird. If you want more, you'll have to increase the amounts yourself.

¼ cup butter
1 #2 can tomatoes, sieved (2 cups)
¼ cup vinegar
3 tablespoons sugar
3 teaspoons paprika
1 small onion, finely diced
2 teaspoons salt
2 teaspoons chili powder
1-½ teaspoons Worcestershire sauce
¼ teaspoon Tabasco® sauce
1 teaspoon black pepper

Mix ingredients in a saucepan and simmer for 15 minutes. Use for basting meat or chicken. Can also be served on the side. Makes enough for 5 pounds of meat or chicken.

Totally Q

More Saucy Suggestions

• Serve all barbecue sauces at room temperature.

• Never serve barbecue sauce in a silver gravy boat.

• Do not apply barbecue sauce while the meat is still on the grill or in the pit.

• At the table, wear sauce protection at all times—a bib with a pig on it is my favorite.

• All barbecue and hot sauces (whether commercial or homemade) should be refrigerated after use. The higher the vinegar content, the longer they will last in the refrigerator; if stored properly, most commercial sauces will be good for several months.

A Basic Recipe for Vinegar BBQ Sauce

Melt half a pound of butter; stir into it a large tablespoon of mustard, half a teaspoonful of red pepper, one of black, salt to taste; add vinegar until the sauce has a strong acid taste. The quantity of the vinegar will depend upon the strength of it. As soon as the meat becomes hot, begin to baste, and continue basting frequently until it is done; pour over the meat any sauce that remains.

Slappin' Fat Bacon Ketchup by Captain Thom's Chili Pepper Company, Baltimore Maryland

There's a guy in Baltimore who makes some pretty interesting and tasty sauces, both barbecue and hot varieties. While the Baltimore area is better known for its blue crabs and seafood than it is hot sauces and barbecue, Captain Thom continues to defy the odds, traveling the country with First Mate Nancy, and plying his wares at various trade shows and exhibitions. Cap'n Thom, as he is more affectionately known locally, came up with this product a few years back and it has been a steady seller ever since. He suggests using it on meatloaf, but I like to smother my burger with it, put it on my fries and have found that it is particularly good as a substitute for regular ketchup in my homemade barbecue sauces. You can find his line of tasty products at www.captainthoms.com

A Chicago-Style Hot Dog in a Bottle

This hot sauce was recently developed by hot sauce man Danny Cash, who called it "Chidawgo." It contains everything you'll find in a Chicago-style hot dog (except the hot dog and roll, of course), and combines the flavors of yellow mustard, green sweet relish, chopped onion, tomato, pickles, two sport peppers and celery salt. The only thing I can say is: Why didn't I think of that?

White Bar-B-Q Sauce?

Big Bob Gibson's Bar-B-Q joint in Decatur, Alabama has been family owned and operated since 1925 and has become a "must visit" for any true barbecue aficionado's bucket list. Their signature dish is barbecued chicken dipped in their

Totally Q

world-famous "white sauce." Unlike other barbecue sauces, the recipe for this elixir includes mayonnaise, horseradish and vinegar. Before you scoff, I suggest you grab yourself a copy of Chris Lilly's book, *Big Bob Gibson's BBQ Book: Recipes and Secrets From a Legendary Barbecue Joint,* and mix up a batch. I'm here to tell you, it brings a very interesting dimension to barbecued chicken. If you ask the folks down Decatur way, they'll tell you that barbecue sauce is *supposed* to be white.

Even BBQ Sauce Has its Limits

Words of wisdom from Barbecue legend Ardie Davis:

"Here's what barbecue sauce *cannot* do for you:

–Convert bad barbecue into good barbecue: if the barbecue is bad, throw it out!

–Erase wrinkles. It can please your palate, but it's not a wonder drug.

–Substitute fake barbecue for real barbecue. The secret to some barbecue may be in the sauce, but if the meat hasn't been cooked with the direct action of fire and smoke, it isn't barbecue."

A Few Words About Sides

According to barbecue pitmaster Myron Mixon, "Everybody knows that man—and woman, for that matter—cannot live by meat alone. That's why God invented side dishes, isn't it?"

Hushpuppies? Wait a Minute, I Thought They Were Shoes!

Most folks agree that Warner Raleigh of North Carolina barbecue fame was one of the first to combine these tasty morsels with barbecued meats back in the 1950s. What is a hushpuppy, you ask? Simply put, it's a deep-fried ball made from corn meal (not to be confused with bull balls, aka Rocky Mountain Oysters). You can make your own or, as is the case with most foods today, puppies are "available frozen in your grocer's freezer section." Although most Southerners worth their weight in corn meal would probably think of you as blasphemous for serving a previously-frozen puppy alongside your 'cue, we all know there are times when the convenience of a ready-to-cook frozen product is the way to go.

Totally Q

Potato Salad, a Dish Best Served at Room Temperature

Wait a minute, did you say room temperature? I thought potato salad was one of those things that had to be kept cold. What about the story where a mess sergeant allegedly poisoned his entire platoon by serving them potato salad that had been kept in a rucksack all day? Most experts say this story is a myth. Today's commercially-made mayonnaise contains pasteurized eggs and acids that actually kill bacteria. Usually, when there comes a case of the trots from eating potato salad at the company barbecue, it is the result of a breakdown on the cook's part.

Let me explain: You're in a rush, you were assigned to bring the potato salad to today's cook-out, and you should have made it yesterday instead of playing golf with your buddies. You are supposed to leave in an hour or so and last week you complained to your wife because SHE was late, so you surely cannot be the cause of a tardy arrival today. You cook the potatoes; they are drained and still steaming. You need to let them cool just like the instructions tell you, but you don't have time, so you toss the spuds around in the colander a few times then call them cooled. Your add the mayonnaise and the rest of the ingredients, stir them up, burp the Tupperware, then dash off to get your shower while your concoction idles on the counter, cooling off.

Wrong.

What you have done here, my friend, has created a bacterial perfect storm. Often this innocent mistake ultimately results in most of the potato salad-eating party guests spending a little more time than usual in the loo the following day...or perhaps worse.

When throwing a BBQ party for the neighbors, it's best to avoid sending them all home with food poisoning. Vintage image courtesy of DivaQ.

Totally Q

Cold mayonnaise added to hot potatoes is a no-no to be avoided at all costs. Follow the directions, don't bend the rules and you'll be fine. Oh. And by the way, after your potato salad has been properly prepared, properly stored and transported to the party, it is best when allowed to come to room temperature before serving. Please keep in mind, if it's 100 degrees in the shade on the day of your company barbecue, this would not be considered "room temperature." You need to use a bit of common sense.

Barbecue's Natural Co-Star

Wilber Shirley sums it up best in a quote found in *Holy Smoke*, a book all about North Carolina barbecue, when he says, "You gotta have coleslaw. I won't even sell somebody a barbecue unless they get coleslaw—there's something wrong with that person. It all goes together." Dr. Bob Sammons, author of *A Spectator's Guide to Competition Barbecue*, tells me that when he feeds folks in Colorado, he will often include a coleslaw selection on the menu. He says people out that way aren't used to seeing slaw, so he includes Wilbur's quote on a sign posted near his buffet line.

The Not-So-Odd Couple: Pickles and 'Cue

Most barbecue joints across America observe tradition by serving some type of a pickle with their barbecue. The combo is a natural. In some restaurants you'll get sliced pickle chips, while in others, it will be whole or a quartered spear. At the famed Arthur Bryant's you can help yourself from a large jar of sliced dill pickle chips located at the end of the counter. While it's unclear where the pairing of pickles and barbecue started, it's a fact that most people enjoy the crunch of a pickle when noshing on 'cue. A few joints down in Texas even tried to add pickle relish to their barbecued beef sandwiches, but this experiment didn't last long.

Top 10 Wines to Drink with BBQ

Most folks don't associate wine with barbecue, but if you find yourself wondering, here is a list of the top ten wines that are recommended, according to the website Gayot (pronounced guy-OH). They are presented in no particular order. When deciding on your food and drink pairings, however, remember the wisdom of Edward Tewkesbury who once said, "Drinking wine with barbecue is pretentious enough without drinking expensive wine."

1) **Woodbridge by Robert Mondavi Brut**: A sparkling California white made from Chardonnay grapes using the Charmat method (don't ask me). To the nose, it brings a hint of citrus, while the taste suggests green apple and lemon.

2) **Grenache Blanc by Tower 15**: A wine with a distinctive herbal flavor that is also well known for its high alcohol content, 14.2 percent to be exact.

3) **Overlook Chardonnay by Landmark Vineyards**: This winery was

Totally Q

founded by a member of the farm equipment manufacturing family, John Deere. This fact alone should make it a very reliable wine.

4) **Big Fire Pinot Gris by R. Stuart & Company**: A sturdy white with hints of apple, ginger and guava.

5) **Uncle Roget's Rosé by Rock Wall**: A California rosé considered dry and fruity, with flavors of strawberry and watermelon.

6) **Clos de los Siete by Michel Rolland**: This red wine is made from a blend of malbec, merlot, cabernet sauvignon, syrah and petit verdot. Noted to be robust and full-bodied. In my view, there's nothing wrong with being full-bodied and robust. At least, I enjoy it.

7) **Arnaldo Caprai by Montefalco Rosso DOC**: A blended Italian red consisting of 70 percent sangiovese, 15 percent sagrantino and 15 percent merlot. A hint of vanilla is also present.

8) **Rioja Reserva by Martin Cendoya**: Aged at least three years inside oak barrels before bottling , this wine is made with grapes grown on vines that are reportedly over one hundred years old.

9) **Hilltop Cabernet Sauvignon by J. Lohr**: A cab from the Paso Robles area of California that is supposed to be a great selection to lay down for a while. This wine also has the distinction of being the most expensive on the list, with a suggested price of $35 per bottle.

10) **Il Raggio del Sole by Castello di Amorosa**: This wine sounds Italian, but it comes from California's Napa Valley. Sweet and low in alcohol, with flavors of orange, peach and honeysuckle.

Wash Down That 'Cue with Fine Swine Wine
NASCAR legend Richard Childress owns and operates a vineyard in Lexington, North Carolina. Each year for the Lexington barbecue festival, he produces a limited local supply of "Fine Swine Wine," which has been described as semisweet with a fruity flavor and would be comfortable being served in a paper cup. In wine jargon, it exhibits hints of cherry and plum with the aroma of cedar and the toastiness of oak. One wine critic said, "It smells like slaw." Another described it as "sweet tea with a kick."

Try Smoking Hard Boiled Eggs, if You Can Keep 'Em Lit
For an interesting twist to your egg salad or any dish containing hard cooked eggs, try this: After boiling and cooling your eggs, crack the shells (without removing them) and toss the eggs into your smoker. Allow the cracked eggs to absorb the smoke for an hour or so before using them in your recipe.

Totally Q

Suggested Fruits for Grilling

Banana: sliced in half lengthwise

Mango; 1/2-inch thick slices

Orange; single sections

Papaya; 1/2- inch thick slices

Peach; 1/2- inch thick slices

Pear; 1/2- inch thick slices

Pineapple; 1/2- inch thick rings

Strawberry; sliced in half

Atomic Buffalo Turds

These little morsels are a very popular appetizer around grills and smokers all across America. You might know them as stuffed jalapeños, hot poppers, poppers, or just ABTs for short. They're made from halved jalapeño peppers that are stuffed, packed or wrapped with just about everything from cream cheese to bacon. I like to take leftover pulled pork, mix it into some softened cream cheese, fill the peppers and then wrap them with bacon. These babies are a real hit. Let your imagination run wild here and your guests will love them. If nothing else, the name will give you some fodder for dinner table discussion.

Moink Balls

This is another very popular barbecued appetizer that—legend has it—originated with Larry Gaian from the really cool website called The BBQ Grail (thebbqgrail.com). A somewhat simple tidbit, it's made by taking a frozen Italian-style meatball that has been thawed, wrapping it with bacon, spearing it with a toothpick and tossing it with your favorite barbecue dry rub. The moink ball then goes into your smoker until the bacon is cooked. The cooked balls can then be dipped into your favorite barbecue sauce before serving and man, are they good. I guess I should warn you, they're habit forming too. Oh, I almost forgot, the name, *moink balls*. Well, the ball part should be obvious, (meatballs), the moink maybe not. Perhaps the formula below will be of help—this is sometimes known as "new math."

Meatball=beef=moo

Bacon= hog= oink

Moo + Oink = Moink

Pig Candy

What could be better than combining the flavors of bacon, sugar and cayenne pepper? We're talking the trifecta here. You can *Google* for an easy recipe, but the concept is very simple. Take some bacon, coat it with brown sugar, dash on some cayenne to your taste, then toss these babies into your smoker or oven on low temp until crispy. Be careful though, because all of that sugar can cause the bacon to become quickly overdone or burnt. When the slices are just right, pull them out and you've got yourself a real tasty treat. One word of caution: You'd better make twice as many as you think you'll need, after all, they ARE pig candy!

Burnt Ends

"That grease hitting those coals makes the smoked flavor...You can't spray it on there, paint it on there, put it on there–that's the natural way to cook it to get the smoke taste." –Wilber Shirley

"Oh, mopping is all right, I suppose. I used to use a mop with lots of lemons in it, and it does give a pork shoulder a nice lemony flavor. But it's not that important. And when you get real busy there just isn't time for it."–Louis Charles Henley

"It is very important that when you put something on the grill, you leave it in place to cook. If you move it around too quickly, chances are it is going to stick."–Bobby Flay

"Barbecue is smoke, and not too much heat, and plenty of time. You can barbecue less-than-choice cuts. You cannot grill them. It takes low heat to tenderize a brisket. Remember that old physics rule. Water boils at 212 degrees. Boil the water out of a tough piece of meat and what have you got? New sandals." –Linda West Eckhardt

"Many grills come with a temperature gauge that reads, 'Smoke, Barbecue, and Grill.' Remove this immediately and throw it as far as you can. Instead, get a thermometer with actual numerical readings, and install it near the cooking grate for the most accurate reading." –Chris Lilly

"Barbecue is, at best, an inexact art. Different woods used for fuel, varying ambient temperatures, changing weather conditions, and the food you're cooking are all part of the equation, and all affect the outcome." –Michael H. Stines, Ph.B.

"Barbecue teaches us to enjoy life not only in self-indulgence, but in self-denial. Once you see the interstitial periods between barbecue as necessary and equally savory, you will gain full mastery over mouth-watering. Or you will be found wanting, and it will kill you. Either way: we're all better off."
–From The Man's Book of BBQ by Brendan McGinley

"Grilling evaporates some of the water in a vegetable, concentrating the flavor. High, dry heat caramelizes natural plant sugars, heightening a vegetable's sweetness. Unlike boiling, which removes flavor from vegetables, grilling seems to intensify their natural taste." –Steven Raichlen

"Just fire and hickory, brick and smoke. Don't spice up nothing." –George Archibald Jr. of Archibald's B.B.Q., Northpoint, Alabama

Cookers and the Fuels That Love Them

There are almost as many different types of cookers, grills and smokers as there are grill masters, and I'm just talking about units that are commercially available, never mind all the homemade devices. Along those lines, innovative folks have constructed cookers out of everything from trash cans to shopping carts. Seems that pretty much any object that won't burn and is large enough to build a fire in has probably been pressed into service at one time or another.

Cooking outdoors can be very habit-forming and prone to triggering unhealthy behaviors such as "cooker hoarding" and the dreaded, "I can grill that" syndrome. For the uninformed, the latter condition has been around about as long as men have congregated around fire pits to watch meat cook, and most of them have been diagnosed with at least a touch of the affliction. It can be defined thusly: A man looks at any type or shape of food, then (with little or no use of brain cells) figures out a way to get said item onto a grill, slather it with sauce and cook it, much to the delight of the other cave dwellers in the village. We can't help ourselves.

I have heard rumors—due at least in part to the recent success of shows like *Pitmasters*—that there has been some talk among television producers about the creation of a new reality show called *Cooker Hoarding*. As we are all painfully aware, most of the standard topics have been covered *ad nauseam*, and while some in the barbecue world are in denial, many others have acknowledged suffering from this malady that is characterized by stockpiling an abundance of cookers. Currently I have nine...or is it ten? Some haven't been used in quite a while, but I just can't part with them. They're like old friends. On some barbecue forums, there are people who actually list their cooker arsenal below their signature, as if somehow they are proclaiming, *"Look how many I have!"* I guess you could say I'm a closet cooker collector because I don't boast about my inventory like that. It all reminds me of that old Johnny Carson/Jack Webb bit about Claude Cooper the kleptomaniac from Cleveland who copped the copper clappers kept in the closet.

Totally Q

Two girls at a hibachi by Kusaakabe Kimbei, 1880.

Hibachi History
The word *hibachi* has its origins in Japan, and loosely translated means "heating vessel" or "fire pot." As is the case with many great products that have been around for a long time, nobody knows exactly when the hibachi was first invented; however, written records suggest that it was in use by the Heian Period (798-1185 A.D.). Because metal was a rare commodity in Japan, early hibachis were carved from cypress wood and lined with clay. Originally used as vessels to carry hot coals for heating the inside of homes, these small fire pits were at some point transformed by a quick-thinking person who added a grate over the top and used the resulting platform to heat tea and to cook small quantities of food. The model familiar to most of us nowadays consists of a two-grate setup. The hibachi's popularity is currently on the upswing, because it provides a great option in situations where larger grills aren't practical or where space is a consideration. In addition, tailgaters have become increasingly fond of the versatility these small but powerful units provide.

Texas Spin Doctors
In Texas in the 1950s and1960s, the barbecue business was wide open as pitmasters and caterers were regularly asked to cook for more and more people. At that time, a fellow by the name of Leonard O'Neill was looking for ways to increase his cooker's output in an attempt to grow his barbecue business. A machinist by trade, he purchased a large rotating oven that had been used by a bread company, made

Totally Q

a few adjustments and converted the unit into a rotating cooker that could handle 3,000 pounds of 'cue at once.

Another Texan named Herbert Oyler was working on a similar development around the same time and created a steel rotisserie pit that was fueled by a wood fire. It's not known whether the two were working together on their projects, if they were in competition, or even if they knew about each other's efforts, but in 1967, Oyler was given a patent for a rotisserie barbecue cooker that is still being manufactured today. In fact, according to the book *Legends of Texas Barbecue*, three of Oyler's units are currently in use at the Houston barbecue joint once owned and operated by Leonard O'Neill.

The Big Green Egg

Ed Fisher was a United States serviceman in the 1950s when he developed a preference for cooking on the domed, ceramic cookers he found while stationed overseas. When he returned home, he began to import the units to sell to his friends and neighbors, but found that the cookers were extremely fragile and did not last long when used regularly and exposed to the elements. Ed began to tinker with various materials and methods, which ultimately resulted in the Big Green Egg, a cooker that is well-known both inside and outside the barbecue world. Ed's designs have now evolved to include five different sizes of eggs, which have spawned an entire nation of "Eggheads." To describe these legions of devotees as committed would be an understatement: They have their own forums, (eggheadforum.com), language (Eggictionary), equipment (Eggcessories), and gatherings, called— of course—"Eggfests." If you ever get the chance, you need to attend one, where you'll see a gaggle of Eggheads smoking and grilling on Big Green Eggs. After that experience, I predict you'll want to become an Egghead too.

Asian-style cookers have come a long way since the hibachi, baby. A Gaggle of BGEs...a gaggle?

123

Totally Q

In Praise of the Ugly Drum
One of the oldest, most-viewed threads on the popular BBQ Brethren Forum is titled simply, *Ugly Drum Smoker*. The thread was started in January 2007, and as of this writing, has received more than 2 million views. This includes 9,000-plus posts covering all aspects of building and using your very own "ugly drum smoker." For those who are wondering what the hell I'm talking about, an ugly drum smoker is a home-built charcoal smoker constructed from a 55-gallon drum and is sometimes known as a UDS for short. If you have a couple of months or so with nothing to do, subscribe to www.bbq-bretheren.com and give this thread a read. I assure you, if you're thinking about building one of these babies, you won't find a better source of information anywhere.

The Jambo
When you see a team pull into a barbecue contest towing a "jambo" pit, you know you're competing against a serious barbecuer. Custom built in Fort Worth, Texas by Jamie Geer, these rigs are used by some of the top teams on the competition barbecue circuit today. Each unit is individually built and looks like a custom car, with its shiny, lustrous finish, chrome wheels, and raised white-letter tires. A Jambo is, as the website proclaims, a true work of art.

This ain't no Texas Tall Tale...this monster smoker rig is for real. You can call him "Cuz."

This One's Big Enough for Texas
Bud Liffick of Houston owns one of the world's largest mobile barbecue pits. Affectionately known as "Cuz," this rig is 80 feet long, weighs 90,000 pounds, has 24 doors (but only one firebox), and can cook between 700 and 900 briskets at once, plus a similar volume of ribs and chicken. Because of its size, Bud uses a semi to take the unit to major barbecue cook-offs, where contestants using it have won major prizes. He told us that it cost $360,000 to build, but some would say it's priceless.

Totally Q

Name That Grill?

Many pitmasters have taken to naming their pits and grills and apparently, the rules are the same as for a ship—female names are preferred. This notion has never really interested me. Don't tell my wife, but I enjoy the peaceful quiet time I spend while tending my cookers. The last thing I want to do is have my cooker sporting a female name and nagging at me while I am trying to barbecue. Consider this quote attributed to an anonymous source: "Shirley treats me right every time. If she weren't a grill, I just might marry her." I don't get it, especially in this case...my mother-in-law's name is Shirley.

What would you name this armadillo-shaped grill...Annie? Arnie? Ashley? Al?

Fast Eddy and the Pellet Poopers...Great Name for a Band

The term *pellet pooper* is used to describe wood pellet-fed barbecue cookers and grills, units that are increasing in popularity every year as their manufacturers hone in on what some would say is "perfection." The cookers are made to run on wood pellets similar to the fuel used in wood pellet heaters in homes all over the country, but the cooking pellets are flavored and are available in all types of wood to impart whatever level of seasoning your little heart desires. Cookshack, Green Mountain Grills (GMG), Traeger, MAK, and Yoder are just a few of the companies producing these units. The folks who cook on them have almost become a cult, much like the stick burners and the ceramic cooker Egghead gang.

Ed "Fast Eddy" Maurin began to manufacture his line of pellet-fueled smokers called Fast Eddy Cookers in 1994 and by 2000, Eddy—who was a fireman, welder and

Totally Q

metal fabricator—had upgraded the unit to include a rotating cooking rack. He later teamed up with Cookshack Inc. of Ponca City, Oklahoma to construct, assemble and distribute the units.

The Weber Kettle—Buoy, What a Cooker!
In 1952, George Stephen was a buoy welder for Weber Brothers Metal Works located just outside of Chicago, Illinois. While preparing to weld the top and bottom halves of a newly created Coast Guard buoy together, he had the brilliant idea of turning the unit into a charcoal cooker. After a bit of trial and error with airflow issues, the Weber Kettle grill was born. In my opinion this innovation contributed greatly to the surge of popularity in outdoor cooking because of its reasonable cost and ease of operation. Weber is also a known leader in the production of high quality gas grills, as well as numerous grilling and smoking accessories.

The Weber Smokey Mountain Model 721001, affectionately known as The Bullet.

The Weber Smokey Mountain
It was 1981 when the Weber Company first introduced Smokey Mountain Cookers to the public. These units were the idea of Erich Schlosser, a senior project engineer for Weber. Initially there were two models: the 1880, which was 14-½ inches in diameter and sold for $100, and the 2880, which measured 18-½ inches across and cost about $120. The 1880 was discontinued in 1983 and the 2880 became known simply as "the WSM" to most of the smoking public. This made things easier because the model numbers changed periodically, from 2880 to 2890, 2820 and then eventually to 721001in 2008. In October of 2008, the model 731001, measuring an expansive 22-1/2 inches in diameter, was introduced with much hoopla. As for making sense of the assigned model numbers...I gave up three sentences ago.

Totally Q

Invasion of the Brazilian Superskewers

Just introduced in 2009, the Carson Rotisserie is a charcoal-fired unit that allows you to spit-roast your meats just like they do in those Brazilian steakhouses. The grill is advertised as portable and folds into its own suitcase-style carrier for a total weight of just over 50 pounds. Don't let the size fool you, however, as the unit also comes with seven skewers, enough to cook a nice-sized load of meat and veggies for your friends. This baby is quickly becoming popular with tailgaters as well because it has a rechargeable battery pack that allows you to spin your spits away from a regular power source—you know, like on a stadium parking lot.

Camerons Stovetop Smoker

Do you want to add a smoky favor to your meal without all the fuss and muss of firing up your large grill or smoker? Would you like to smoke meat indoors without making your house smell like...well, a smokehouse? Then you need to check out this super handy stove top smoker that's manufactured right here in the U S of A—in Colorado, to be specific. The whole thing weighs 8 pounds and is about the size of a large sauce pan but there is also a mini smoker that weighs only 3 pounds and is perfect for two. Either unit can be used on the stovetop or outside on the grill and produces its smoke with finely ground wood chips that come in a variety of flavors. The best part, however, is that when you are done, the whole thing fits into the dishwasher for easy cleanup.

Cobb Tabletop Grill

This is the perfect fit for anyone concerned about space when buying an outdoor grill, smoker, oven or fryer. The Cobb is a portable stainless steel unit that weighs approximately 11 pounds and comes with its very own carrying case, two features that have increased its popularity with the tailgating crowd. The manufacturer says it will cook for over three hours on only eight to 10 charcoal briquettes and is able to heat up to 450 degrees F, which make this one of the most efficient and versatile portable outdoor cookers available today.

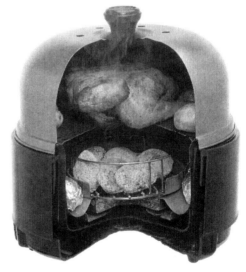

The award-winning design of the Cobb Grill makes for a compact, easy-to-clean unit.

Totally Q

Grilling No-Man's Land

I have always been a fan of the mantra, "have grill, will travel." In other words, grill anywhere, everywhere and wherever. Ray Lampe, better known as Dr. BBQ, makes a few good suggestions in his book *Barbecue All Year Long*, for a few places that should be avoided when firing up your grill or smoker:

• Someone else's private property
• Landfills
• Cemeteries
• Swamps
• Dark alleys
• Chemical dumps
• Death Valley in the summertime
• Near packs of roving wild dogs

While these are all good suggestions, I just couldn't help but come up with a few more, which would include:

• Gas stations (for obvious reasons).
• In the direct path of a land falling hurricane (75+ mph winds are just a bit much).
• On the deck of a Bering Sea crab boat (while underway in a 30-foot sea).
• On the altar during your best friend's wedding.
• At a vegan rally (I think I would rather grill at a gas station).
• Spot-a-pots or latrines (lack of ambiance).
• At a bluegrass festival when located upwind from the performing band. I have done this. As the smoke wafted down and enveloped the band, I heard more than a few snide comments and received plenty of dirty looks. My suggestion here would be to wait until the band takes a break, then invite them to join you for lunch.
• Aboard a transcontinental flight (all flights are non-smoking these days).
• While riding on the A train in New York City (that is of course, unless you are in the smoking car).
• In sporting event parking lots designated as "No Tailgating" (this is self-explanatory).

Totally Q

The Lowdown on Fuels

Startin' Your Fire

The debate continues to rage concerning the use of charcoal lighter fluid products, as well as briquettes infused with chemical fire accelerants. I'm neither a scientist nor a raving greeniac, but I have to tell you, there's just something unnatural about using these products. It kind of reminds me of toasting a marshmallow or hot dog over a fire made with those fake fireplace logs. You've seen them—you light the paper on the outside and they burn for an hour or two. I don't think I'd want to be eating anything cooked over one of those babies. Suffice it to say, there are scads of fire-starting alternatives on the market today that are just as easy and efficient as lighter fluid and my personal preference is the charcoal chimney. It may be a little slower than fluid, but there's definitely less chemical involvement, and when we're talking about a nice

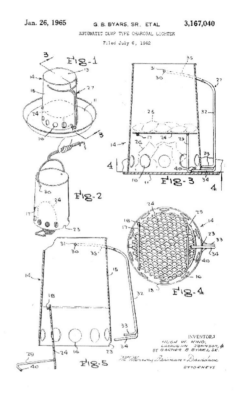

A 1965 patent application drawing for a charcoal starter.

steak or a piece of prime seafood, the fewer chemicals, the better.

Gas is Good

Many self-proclaimed barbecue purists look down their smoke-filled noses at anyone who would dare to cook or grill on a gas-fired unit. For the life of me, I don't see why. As far as I'm concerned, it's just another tool in my arsenal of outdoor cooking weapons. In fact, I have several cookers: some are wood-fueled, some burn charcoal, and some are fueled by—I'm not ashamed to say—GAS! I will also tell you, that if someone were tracking my habits, they would find that my gasser probably gets the most consistent use out of all the cookers I own.

Totally Q

More Than 16 Tons

Industry sources estimate that Americans buy in excess of 884,000 tons of charcoal briquettes in any given year, which are then used in the grills owned by more than 84 percent of all households.

Don't Get Bitten by the Mesquite Bug

There are reports from North Carolina that several colonies of scorpions have been discovered in close proximity to barbecue joints and it's suspected that the critters hitchhiked to the state inside loads of mesquite wood.

While there are likely some folks who would rid the Tar Heel state of mesquite altogether because of this bug invasion, Lorenzo Vences, the pitmaster at Cooper's Old Time Pit Bar-B-Q in Llano, Texas, believes it is worth keeping around. "Mesquite," he says, "gives the meat a lot of flavor without over smoking it."

Fueling the Fire, 1950s-Style

The 1951 *Sunset Barbecue Cookbook* offers some sage advice as to which woods to avoid when barbecuing. "Some kinds are too zestful; eucalyptus gives meat a medicinal flavor, pine imparts a turpentine taste." I can understand the reasoning behind avoiding a medicinal taste; we have all tasted medicines with an unpleasant flavor, although that happens much less today than it did 30 years ago. But the rest of the statement got me to wondering: *How in the world did the author know what turpentine tastes like?*

Later on in the same book we are told, "Paper and kindling will usually coax charcoal into flame, but sometimes more encouragement is needed. Pine chips or kindling sticks are effective, as are various inflammable liquids, such as alcohol, antifreeze, kerosene, diesel fuel, white gasoline, or commercially made lighter solutions." Wow, I don't even know where to begin here—didn't they just tell us a few paragraphs ago to avoid using pine? As for tossing any inflammable liquids, let's just say: DO NOT USE ANY OF THESE AFORMENTIONED LIQUIDS WHEN STARTING YOUR COOKING FIRE...OR ANY FIRE, FOR THAT MATTER. The only exception would be lighter fluid. While this product is still widely available, there are many folks today

Totally Q

who would advise against its use. Things were different back in the 50s, however, and I love the last line of the paragraph in this treatise on fuels, which reads: "These solutions should be allowed to burn off completely, however, otherwise they may impart a disagreeable taste to the meat." May impart?

Burnt Ends

"The type of pit you use is less critical than your willingness to learn to cook with it. A recent visitor to my patio summed it up well: 'Basically, barbecue is simply stewardship of the fire.' How true! I know one guy who won the most prestigious barbecue cook-off in Texas on a #3 washtub. Unfortunately, experience with a given pit is the only true teacher." —Red Caldwell

"Getting fancy on the grill is like playing leapfrog with a unicorn. It never works." —From the *Marlboro Cook Like a Man Cookbook* by Phillip Morris

"There's nothing worse than trying to cook for a crowd on too small a grill." —Klaus Marx

"I'll put my grilling up against anybody's. I am the grill master!" —Si Robertson, Duck Commander/Duck Dynasty

"There's an old Smokey Mountain tradition: when you build something, you build it to last. Now there's a smoke cooker worthy of that timeless tradition. You'll love what it does to fish, meat and game...season after season, year after year." —Weber Smokey Mountain Cooker Owner's Manual, 1981

"Grills in the wild live in matriarchal clans of up to 50. Scientists are debating whether to refer to them as flocks, prides, or just a really good time." —From *The Man's Book of the BBQ* by Brendan McGinley

"You know you've gone too far when you turn your fireplace into a BBQ pit." —From the *Marlboro Cook Like a Man Cookbook* by Phillip Morris

"Grill it. Smoke it. BBQ the heck out of it." —*From the Marlboro Cook Like a Man Cookbook* by Phillip Morris

"Don't worry about buying a big fancy smoker, you can make great barbecue on a Weber, if you know what you are doing."

Totally Q

—Harley Goerlitz, "The Winningest Barbecuer in Texas," whose cooker of choice was a homemade unit cobbled together using an old oil drum.

"I love using gas grills because they are easier to heat and it's much easier to control the flames with a gas grill than with a charcoal fire. Grilling is not just about lighting a fire." —Bobby Flay

With a cute little table-top smoker like this one, you'll be tempted to BBQ anywhere. Photo courtesy of George Hensler

Talk about a winning combination: booze and 'cue. This enormous Jack Daniel's bottle is actually a smoker. Photo by Mike Stines, courtesy of Sunbelt Archives.

10 Forums, Publications, Societies & Sites

So, you want to learn how to cook good barbecue or grill a top-notch steak? All you have to do is Google it. This is something we have come to take for granted. It wasn't that long ago when you had to ask a friend, read a magazine article or go to your local library and check out an (extremely outdated) book to find the answers you needed.

Today, the world is at our fingertips, particularly in regard to outdoor cooking. With minimal effort, you can find the answer to just about any question without even changing out of your pajamas. Heck, with iPads and smartphones, you can search for information and never leave your grill or smoker.

On the Web, there are many forums and sites offering tons of information ripe for the picking. While it's a well-known fact that some of the content on the Internet is complete crap, the majority of what's out there is extremely helpful. Step-by-step instructions, videos, recipes...it's all there for the asking. There are a multitude of groups, bloggers, gangs and companies out in hyperspace just waiting to offer you advice, sell you something, or thoroughly confuse you. As with anything, be sure to use your mind filter and consider the source. In my opinion the info is pretty damn good overall.

Forums

The First Barbecue Blogger?
Charles Lamb (1775-1834) was an essayist who lived in merry old England. From what I can determine, he published many works relating to food and dining in his day. One of his most popular pieces is titled *A Dissertation Upon Roasted Pig*, which was first published in 1904. It goes without saying that Lamb's blog about pulled pork predates the Internet—never mind the word *blog*—by a couple of hundred years.

Totally Q

Brothers in Smoke

On March 11, 2003, a New Yorker named Phil Rizzardi (along with about 40 of his closest Internet friends) started a splinter *Yahoo* chat group called the Bandera Brethren, a forum where people interested in outdoor cooking could share information and experiences in relation to this increasingly popular pursuit. As news of their newly-formed community spread, they quickly realized that their initial system would

not support the growth or improvements they wanted to make, so Phil worked with the gang to develop and implement a new and expanded site which they renamed The BBQ Brethren Forum (www.bbq-brethren.com) and launched just five months after introducing the first site. The goal of this group is neatly summed up by Phil, or the Grand Poobah, as he is affectionately known on the forum, who declared, "The overall goal for The Brethren is the promotion of BBQ and the camaraderie that comes with it."

The First Forum

The BBQ Forum (www.thebbqforum.com) was started in 1995 by Ray Basso, who says it began as a project on the Kansas City Bar-B-Que Connections site. Many believe this was the first Internet page to deal specifically with barbecue. Ray began the forum to give folks a way to communicate and trade secrets and tips, and it has

since received posts from many of the Who's Who in today's barbecue world. I find it interesting that these folks are not only posting, but freely dispensing advice, something just not seen much in today's dollar-driven society. As a result of its popularity, The Forum's archives now contain an extensive collection of recipes, tips and tidbits pertaining to all types of outdoor and indoor cooking. From its humble beginnings (when a mere 60 messages were posted), The Forum has seen a steady rise in posts and visits, and will continue to move the spirit of barbecue well into the future.

Forum Handles We Like:
Pigosaurus Rex • BeerBQue • The Pig Lebowski
Bar-B-Sue • PatioDaddio • PiggieSmallz • SaucyWench

Totally Q

Pellet Head Forum

My name is _____ and I am a pellet smoker.

This is how visitors are first introduced to PelletSmoking.com, a forum dedicated to folks with an interest in—you guessed it—wood pellet cookers and smokers. Providing a place for Pelletheads (as they have named themselves) to trade secrets and tips, the site has developed a cult-like following, all in the quest for that perfect 'cue.

Websites

Amazing Ribs

Craig "Meathead" Goldwyn runs this site, and in my humble opinion, it's one of the most informative barbecue/grilling sources on the Web. With all the product reviews, techniques, recipes, articles and other information, you could spend days here and never read the same thing twice. If you have a week or so with nothing to do, or are looking for any and all barbecue information, you need to check out this site at www.amazingribs.com.

Diva Q

Danielle Bennett Dimovski is known to most in the barbecue world as Diva Q. This girl is a walking, talking, barbecue machine from Barrie, Ontario. Don't let the fact that she's from Canada fool you—Diva knows her 'cue inside and out. A wife and mother of three, Diva probably gets more done before putting her kids on the bus in the morning than most of us do all day long. She's trying new recipes, testing products, blogging, reviewing restaurants, filming TV spots, hawking for her sponsors and giving cooking demos and classes. Her blog site is full of great recipes, tips and other good barbecue information and best of all, the information and commentary is always fresh and up-to-date at www.divaq.ca.

Totally Q

Grilling With Rich

This fairly new site was launched in 2010 by Richard Wachtel from the Washington, D.C. area, and is just chock full of useful information about all types of outdoor cooking. Reviews, how-to's, interviews...it's all here in a sort of one-stop-shop. Even though

Rich is the new guy on the block, he really knows how to build a site that delivers: www. grillingwithrich.com.

For Men Only: Man B Que

There is a fairly new site at manbque.com that promotes meat, beer and rock and roll—how can you go wrong? Below is a small snippet from their mission statement:

"Man B Que has room for everyone, from master grillers to backyard novices. Anyone who shows up is guaranteed an evening of amazing food and great times, regardless of prior grilling experience or skill level. There's room for everyone, provided they're in possession of a Y chromosome. As the name suggests, Man B Que MEATings are currently male-only. We hope this comes across as charming and retro, not sexist. Despair not, fairer sex, our Man B Que Events are open to YOU. Finally, a place for those wonderful ladies that think grills are sexy and who would throw a roundhouse punch at anyone who attempts to serve them a cosmopolitan."

The site also includes some hilarious rules (I'm not making this stuff up) for Man B Que, which are listed as follows:

1) Only men attend Man B Que.

2) Vegetarians are not allowed at Man B Que. (Unless they bring us meat...or allow us to throw tomatoes and eggs at them.)

3) Any vegetables served at Man B Que must be within the tight parameters of meat in the form of a kabob.

4) Man B Que should only be held during the week. Weekends are for Coed B

Ques, where there is a slight chance of actually going home with a woman.

5) No less than four different meats are to be served at Man B Que.

Totally Q

There is a maximum of 17-½ meats allowed. Processed meats such as non-beef hot dogs and gyro meat count as a ½-meat.

6) You must bring enough meat to share with fellow Man B Que attendees...Unless you killed it, then you can bring the one piece for yourself.

7) You must also bring enough beers to share. Trading of beers is only allowed if beers being traded are of equal value and taste. Be aware that your beer is a reflection of you and you will probably be judged based on your selection.

8) The grill at the Man B Que must always be in use, with no less than 3 pieces of meat being cooked.

9) Loose fitting attire is encouraged at Man B Que; sweatpants or basketball shorts being the suggested attire.

10) Pets are allowed at Man B Que; pit bulls, dinosaurs, gorillas and great white sharks being the preferred variety.

11) Swords and power tools are encouraged to be on hand at Man B Que, but not necessary.

12) There shall be no use of utensils at Man B Que, unless it's a grilling tool.

13) You must shout at Man B Que.

14) Always exaggerate at Man B Que.

15) There is no asking at Man B Que; there is only taking.

16) The only accepted greeting, form of encouragement or sign of appreciation at Man B Que is a shout of "MAN B QUE!"

17) Guests at Man B Que must directly be invited by a presiding member of the Man B Que committee. If not invited, aspiring guests must attempt to bribe the committee with alcohol, meat or gold. (This will not guarantee entry into Man B Que, but it's a start.)

18) When referring to a female life partner, a woman you are currently having "relations" with, a woman who has borne your spawn or any other woman (not blood related) whom you let into your living space more than twice a week, you must refer to this woman as "My Old Lady."

19) No emotions shall be present at Man B Que**. This being said, insults, false accusations and any other derogatory comments aimed at Man B Que invitees are strongly encouraged.

**Accepted emotions: Euphoric happiness and enjoyment brought on by mass alcohol and/or meat consumption, hate and disgust.

Totally Q

YouTube and Google

I once had a great idea to license the domain name www.quetube.com that would be used for video clips on all things barbecue. As always, I was a few days late and a couple of dollars short, and from what I can tell, the site is taken but not in use...maybe someday. But, not to worry, there is always You Tube (www.youtube.com) where the cooking world is at your fingertips 24/7 and there are clips for almost anything you would ever want to see when it comes to barbecuing, grilling or outdoor cooking, as well as quite a few that most folks wouldn't want to see. But hey, to each his own. I plugged in "prepping a brisket," for example, and received multiple hits, but even if the information you are after is not available on YouTube, all you have to remember is this: *Google is your friend.* When I punched in "Preparing a brisket" on this search engine, it generated more than 328,000 possibilities. These days, there's just no excuse for ignorance.

BBQTV

This site at www.bbqtv.com was started in the 1980s by a certified national barbecue judge named Marc Farris, who realized that barbecue was increasing in popularity and there was a real thirst for related knowledge.. The site currently has over 650 hours of online programming that is watched by more than 5 million viewers from around the world. Video clips cover subjects that include equipment talk, cooking demonstrations, barbecue restaurant visits and up-to-date competition coverage.

BBQ Superstars

This cool site is run by Darryl Mast, and includes film clips, interviews and on-the-scene reporting from around the barbecue world. Darryl also hosts a weekly Internet radio show with guests who include anyone involved in the pursuit of 'cue, from recent contest winners to sauce makers and pit builders. Check it out at www.bbqsuperstars.com.

Barbecue Radio

Internet radio has really taken off in the past few years, and—wouldn't you know it—there's a barbecue presence riding right along. One of the forerunners of this wave is Greg Rempe, host of the *Barbecue Central Radio Show* at www.thebbqcentralshow.com. He is

Totally Q

heard weekly on the Outdoor Cooking Channel at www.outdoorcookingchannel. com, which is a great place to hear shows, see clips, get tips and generally immerse yourself in the realm of outdoor cookery. Greg's guests range from the most recent contest winners to TV producers, equipment designers and manufacturers.

Huck's Hut
Another regular on the Outdoor Cooking Channel is Bruce "Huck Jr." McCall and his show *In the Hut*. This show is broadcast biweekly and usually includes a lively panel discussion about many aspects of barbecue. Huck Jr. also hosts a great website that includes barbecue product reviews, video clips, and a ton of information about the world of 'cue.

Barbecue and Social Media

It goes without saying that there's a huge barbecue presence on most social media outlets. You can access contest results on Facebook see them on Twitter as they are being announced or look through pictures of folks grilling and smoking which are posted regularly for all to see. It's pretty neat stuff if you're into it, but if you aren't, you probably wouldn't be reading this now, would you?

What you might not be aware of is the fact that barbecue has its own social network at www.bbqbackyard.com. This site was the brainchild of Heath Hall and Brett Thompson of Pork Barrel BBQ, and Rod Gray of Pellet Envy BBQ, all of whom a recognized the potential for a more detailed and barbecue-specific social media networking venue. Together, these guys launched their BBQ Pitmaster Social Network in February of 2011, a forum that currently has more than 3,700 members, with more signing up each day. Among other things, the site makes it possible to create your own page, where you're free to post your own barbecue pictures and videos; currently, there are more than 10,000 member-posted photographs available for viewing. The site also hosts group chats featuring many of the Who's Who in the barbecue world who answer questions and offer tips and suggestions for improving your outdoor cooking experience. There are topics of interest for everyone, from the serious competition cook to the backyard beginner,

Totally Q

in addition to a large collection of video clips featuring "how to" instructions, assorted personal interviews and barbecue-related discussions.

Publications

The Kansas City Barbecue Society *Bullsheet*

The *Bullsheet* is a monthly tabloid newspaper published by the Kansas City Barbecue Society (KCBS). The "newsletter," as it was known in the beginning, was launched during the formation of KCBS and originally provided the main draw for membership, with information on contest results and upcoming events. The newsletters initially were mailed periodically, but clamor from the growing membership called for more information and regularity. As a result, the *Bullsheet* grew from a modest, two-sided newsletter to an official tabloid and the content was expanded to now include information on personalities, recipes, cooking techniques, events outside the Kansas City area and recent contest results. In 1988, the KCBS membership was 800 and growing, so the founding committee decided to hire a full-time editor. Today the *Bullsheet* is usually around 50 pages long and is mailed to more than 13,000 members monthly. If you add the family memberships and online subscriptions, the paper is read by about 16,000 people a month. That's not too bad!

The National Barbecue News

The *National Barbecue News* is a monthly publication that was first distributed in February 1990 in Douglas, Georgia to cover all aspects of the barbecue world, including competitions, catering, equipment, restaurants and general information. It was created by Dr. Donald and Frances Gillis, along with their friends Joe and Carlene Phelps, all longtime friends who had competed in barbecue contests under the team name The Smoke House. The Phelpses eventually bought out the Gillises in 1999 and ran the paper until 2003 when they sold their interest to their son,

140

Totally Q

Kell, who runs the publication today. Considered a leader in the barbecue world, the *National Barbecue News* currently has a total circulation of more than 8,000, with subscribers in 16 foreign countries. The publication also hosts an authoritative website at www.BarbecueNews.com.

Societies and Associations

The Kansas City Barbeque Society (KCBS)

This Society was formed back in 1986 by three friends as they sipped a few drinks and discussed a favorite subject—barbecue. Carolyn and Gary Wells and longtime friend Rick Welsh had been cooking at local barbeque contests in the Kansas City area for a few years and noticed that the competitions lacked consistency and organization, and that the rules were different every time they cooked. *There has to be a better way,* they thought. As a result, they started a club for cookers which had an initial membership of 30, each of whom paid $30 in annual dues. The group's mantra was, "It just doesn't matter," and the only requirement

KANSAS CITY
BARBEQUE
★ S O C I E T Y ★

for membership was an agreement to take nothing seriously. By 1987, membership had increased to 168 and the group began receiving requests to "sanction" some of the contests that already existed. It wasn't long before they became the KCBS and instituted various methods and procedures for cooking and judging barbeque contests, including a computerized score tabulation program. In 1988, KCBS released a cookbook titled *The Passion of BBQ*, which contained member recipes and tips and reportedly sold 3,500 copies in its first month of release. Today, the Kansas City Barbeque Society boasts more than 14,000 members worldwide and is expecting to sanction more than 300 contests around the country. This is an impressive accomplishment for a group that was founded on the saying, "It just doesn't matter." I guess it really *does*!

KCBS By The Numbers

Courtesy of Kelly Cain, editor of the monthly KCBS publication the *Bullsheet*, here are a few statistics for your reading enjoyment: In 2011, there were 380 KCBS-sanctioned contests held throughout the country and in February 2012, 372 were already on the schedule. As of 2012, there were 15,821 paid members, which included 11,427 certified barbecue judges. In 2011, KCBS held 66 classes at various locations to teach folks the fine points and procedures for judging a KCBS barbecue contest.

Totally Q

Missionaries of Meat
This is the mission statement of KCBS: "Our mission is to celebrate, teach, preserve, and promote barbeque as a culinary technique, sport and art form. We want barbeque to be recognized as America's Cuisine."

NBBQA
The National Barbecue Association was founded in 1991 to address the needs of the broad, diverse and growing barbecue industry. When formed, there was no single voice representing the overall barbecue industry. Since its inception, the organization has grown to more than 2,000 members from all over the barbecue spectrum.

NATIONAL BARBECUE ASSOCIATION

Caterers, restaurateurs, equipment suppliers, rub and sauce makers, competitors, backyard cooks and folks wanting to learn how to 'cue are all welcome under the large tent of the National Barbecue Association. Their mission statement is as follows: "Sharing and expanding the diverse culture of barbecue through networking and education."

In addition, the NBBQA has an inclusive vision statement to help promote the more enjoyable aspects of our favorite activity: "Our vision is an expansive barbecue community that embraces all things barbecue—from low and slow to grilling, catering to competing, or simply the fun and friendship of a backyard cookout." Now that's a vision I can sink my teeth into.

Mid Atlantic Barbecue Association
The Pennsylvania Barbecue Association was formed as a nonprofit corporation in

2004 and the name was changed to the Mid Atlantic Barbecue Association in 2005 by the group's first president, James H. Noon. The organization's mission statement is the same today as when it was first formed, pledging "to promote interest in all aspects of barbecuing." Currently, this group has more than 250 members who are involved in all levels of 'cue, from backyard cookers and competition pitmasters to caterers and restaurant owners.

The Florida Bar-B-Que Association
Formed in the year 2000 by a small group of competition barbecue cooks and

Totally Q

judges (as well as a few other interested parties), the Florida Bar-B-Que Association (FBA) has grown from its humble beginnings to 500-plus members today. In the year 2011, the association sanctioned 34 contests all over the southeastern section of the United States. Some of the major differences between the FBA and other sanctioning bodies include procedural items such as allowing one hour between turn-ins, forbidding garnish in the turn-in boxes and mandating that every judge's score is always counted.

Joe Cahn, Official Old COOT

Joe is the self-proclaimed Commissioner of Tailgating, who runs a cool website at www.tailgating.com. He has spent many years visiting collegiate and professional sports venues around the country collecting tailgating information and facts for use by sports fans. During his quest, Joe has racked up more than 500,000 miles on his vehicles and has attended more than 500 tailgate parties while visiting 31 professional and 123 college stadiums. How's that for a great gig?

Burnt Ends

"Pride, more than anything else—more, even than profit—is what keeps them standing watchfully over the fires. Pride and honesty and stubbornness compel them to do it right, or quit doing it."—John Edgerton

"All barbecue is local. It's a performance art enacted by one pitmaster, with a specific combination of setting, ingredients, goals, customers...Even a brick-by-brick transplant of the really good joints to, say, the Cours Napoleon or the Louvre, with the same pitmaster as a curator and all the ingredients flown in on Air France, wouldn't, wouldn't be the same." —Raymond Sokolov

"Like a fine wine, good barbecue should pass the lips with a tang, roll around in the mouth with flavorful finesse, disappear down the throat and leave behind only a light sensation of having been there."—Larry Cheek

Totally Q

"Beer can chicken— just another excuse to get your wife to buy you a 12 pack..."
—Solidkick from The BBQ Brethren Forum

"When people come over to your house, don't just sling food at them. Let them see you work. Let them see that you know what you are doing. Then go have some drinks around the pool and relax."—Myron Mixon

"O father, the pig, the pig, do come and taste how nice the burnt pig eats."
—Spoken by Bo-bo, the great lubberly boy in *A Dissertation Upon Roast Pig*, an essay written by Charles Lamb in 1904

"Once you make a decision to BBQ from your heart (i.e., intention), and not your brain (i.e., expectation), the universe will conspire to make your wishes come into reality." —Pitmaster Harry Soo of Slap Yo Daddy BBQ Team

"How do I feel about cooking chicken at a barbecue competition? I can sum it up pretty easily: I hate it. This has nothing to do with the way it tastes—I love to eat it. But it's the toughest damn category in competitive barbecue. Comparatively, chicken takes a lot of preparation time and it's the most tedious work. I can prep all of my other categories, including a whole hog, in less time than it takes me to prep chicken."
—Myron Mixon

Ray "Dr. BBQ" Lampe trimming chicken in his trailer at a BBQ competition.
Photo courtesy of Dr. BBQ.

Joints & Dives: Finding Great 'Cue

f you drive into most towns and ask one of the local denizens where the nearest pizzeria is located, often you'll get nothing but a blank stare or maybe a shoulder shrug. If you ask that same person where you can get yourself a good plate of barbecue, chances are you'll not only get a recommendation, but you might even get directions and some suggestions on what to order.

People know their 'cue, and most times they are more than just a little bit loyal and proud of the unique offerings within their communities. This chapter contains a few tips for when you're on the road and jonesin' for some barbecue, along with a small sampling of the thousands of joints that dot our country—I even found a fly-in barbecue restaurant! From the busy streets of New York to the wide open plains of Texas and everywhere in between, no matter where you are, your next barbecue adventure is never far away.

Holy Pork!
Bob Garner remembers when barbecue joints were rare and special places: "In earlier days, the names of pioneering restaurateurs were spoken in reverent tones, usually by the males of the family, and the infrequent meal at one of those hallowed establishments was something like worshiping in church, as eyes closed and heads shook slowly and wordlessly back and forth over the evidence of grace bestowed in the form of peppery, chopped pork. In the intervals between such rites, frequent reminiscing no doubt elevated the quality of the barbecue to mythical proportions."

BBQ and Health Departments—Like Oil and Water
I've heard stories in which health department officials have "grandfathered in" a noncompliant operation and allowed it to stay open simply because it has been in place for 20 or 30 years. If the place is sold, however, the new owners will have to spend thousands of dollars to upgrade. Seems that many barbecue joints are constantly fighting with the local health department because barbecue, by its very nature, is an undertaking best suited for the great outdoors. Purveyors of smoked

Totally Q

meat products often construct lean-to's, side porches or makeshift roofs to cover their cookers in the event of foul weather and to facilitate nighttime operations, but these setups are often frowned upon by local health inspectors. Seems that the old-time methods of the best barbecue cooking simply cannot be adapted to satisfy a modern checklist and there are some who even insist that the best 'cue is found in those places that have the most problems with the health department.

Never Say Never, When it Comes to 'Cue
According to Greg Johnson and Vince Staten, "Barbecue lovers love to make barbecue rules. Never go in a barbecue joint that has a gas pump outside. Never go in a barbecue joint that sells hamburgers. Never go in a barbecue joint that's nicer looking than your house. Never eat at a barbecue joint that has its own T-shirts. But for every rule there is an exception."

This great vintage photo shows an old BBQ joint near Fort Benning, Georgia.
Courtesy of Sunbelt Archives

Pass the Plate
Many barbecue joints, especially some that have been around for a while, serve their offerings on nothing but a sheet of butcher paper. This may have been okay 50 years ago because it was cheap, readily available, and folks didn't much care. In today's world, however, I think most of us would rather use a plate. And is providing a few utensils too much to ask? Consider the opinion of John Raven, a.k.a. Daredevil Bad McFad, who is known to his friends as just plain Bad. "One problem I have with

146

Totally Q

just about all the barbecue joints I have visited is that unforgivable butcher paper. I take my brisket to the table, and by the time I have cut one or two slices I am eating through the hole in the butcher paper and onto the top of a table that could use a good steam cleaning. I want a real plate, and I want a real fork. I carry a knife."

Best Joints in the World?
A website called The Best Barbecue Joints From Around the World, (did you expect anything else?) has put together the following list, which I've included here—in no particular order:

Arthur Bryant's, Kansas City, Missouri
The Pit, Raleigh, North Carolina
Kreuz Market, Lockhart, Texas
Lambert's Downtown Barbecue, Austin, Texas
17th Street Bar & Grill, Murphysboro, Illinois
Oklahoma Joe's, Kansas City, Kansas

Holy Barbecue, Batman!
When two brothers decided to open Bat's BBQ in Rock Hill South Carolina, they combined their initials to form the name of the restaurant: Beau And Travis, abbreviated to BAT. They were moving right along, making and selling their 'cue, when they decided it might be a good idea to trademark their business name.

In the spring of 2010, they applied to the U.S. Patent Office in Washington, D. C. through all the proper channels and anxiously awaited approval. They assumed everything was going well...right up to the point they received a cease-and-desist letter from DC Comics, the holder of the Batman trademark. Talk about gumming up the works.

Most times, when a large entity like DC Comics flexes its legal muscle, the company on the receiving end cowers, concedes, rolls over, and complies. That's just the way it is in corporate America today. It's often better to run for cover and avoid a long, drawn out, and very expensive litigious *tête á tête*, in which the lawyers are the only real winners.

In this case, however, the brothers Broussard have elected to fight and have hired an attorney and are preparing their arguments. All I can say is, *Holy Barbecue, Batman!* I wonder how this battle will turn out. I guess it's no secret that I'm pulling for the underdogs in this epic battle. Sock! Bam! Boom! To find out who wins, tune in next week, same bat-time, same bat-channel. Oops, I'd better be careful—I'll bet that phrase is trademarked, too!

Totally Q

Alabama barbecue scene, circa 1925. The more things change, the more they stay the same. Thanks, Abe! Courtesy of Sunbelt Archives.

We Can Thank Abe Lincoln for Southern BBQ
According to the book, *Legends of Texas Barbecue:* "After emancipation, African Americans from East Texas and the rest of the South gravitated to large cities. In every city of size, they established at least one outpost of southern-style barbecue. Many of these black urban barbecue joints were justly famous for their ribs. A few of them have become legendary institutions that are considered treasures by their hometowns." Now that's a positive perk of the Emancipation Proclamation that nobody was expecting.

Wait A Minute...Shouldn't He Be Driving a Really Fast Car?
When NASCAR legend David Pearson got a hankering for a plate of North Carolina barbecue, he jumped in his private helicopter for a quick trip to Alston Bridges Barbecue in Shelby. Once there, he landed the chopper in a nearby parking lot, walked in, had his lunch and flew home. Now that's what I call express 'cue.

The Infamous Ribless McRib Sandwich
Since 1981, the McRib sandwich has been making an occasional appearance (with much fanfare, of course) at a McDonald's Restaurant near you. A rib sandwich

Totally Q

without a rib bone...*WTF?* There has been much discussion as to what is actually *in* a McRib sandwich, so to satisfy your hunger for such trivial knowledge, here is what McDonald's says on its website: "McRib Pork Patty: Pork, water, salt, dextrose, preservatives BHA, propyl gallate, citric acid." BHA is better known as butylated hydroxyanisole, and is used to help prevent fats from going rancid. Propyl gallate is used to protect oils and fats found in many products from oxidation; it can also be found in lubricants, cosmetics and hair products.

I guess I can live with those additives; they're probably in any fast food sold by the ton across America today. The question I have is this, *How exactly do they define "pork"?* Somehow, I don't think it's a slab of spares or baby backs with the bone removed, cut into serving sized potions, then slapped on a bun with some reconstituted onions, sliced pickles and barbecue sauce. Maybe I don't want to know—after all, sometimes ignorance really is bliss. What might not be so blissful, however, is that a single McRib sandwich contains 500 calories and 26 grams of fat, so if I need a reason not to order one, the caloric overload excuse should suffice. After all, I do have my svelte figure to consider.

Is Computerized 'Cue In Your Future?

Here's a great excerpt from the book *Legends of Texas Barbecue* that describes one of the down sides of modernization: "As small town retail districts fade away, some of the oldest barbecue joints in Texas have closed their doors or moved to greener pastures. Meanwhile, in urban Texas strip malls, new barbecue restaurants are decorated to look like old country stores. The high school kids that work there probably don't even know why. In these new automated operations, employees load meat onto racks of gas-fired rotisserie ovens, push a button, and go home. The virtual barbecue oven does the rest. The quality of the smoked meat pales in comparison to the taste of meat cooked the old-fashioned way with nothing but smoke."

Myrtle's Heavenly Sauce Recipe Went With Her

Myrtle Miller Johnson was the proprietor, pitmaster, head cook and bottle washer at Miller's Bar-B-Q in San Antonio, Texas. Her father Harvey started the business in 1941, selling sandwiches from his backyard barbecue pit for 15 cents apiece. He never advertised or took out a Yellow Pages ad, but was known to have some of the best 'cue in town for almost 50 years. Some say that even though the restaurant operated in violation of modern-day zoning and health department regulations, county officials privately agreed that the establishment was too important to the city of San Antonio to bother issuing any notices.

When the business closed its doors in 1990, Myrtle told a reporter during an

Totally Q

interview that for years, folks had been after her to give up her family's secret barbecue sauce recipe. She said that despite offers to purchase the formula, she never even considered selling the recipe she had devised along with her mother and father back in the early years of operation.

What's more, she had given instructions that if she were to die while the joint was still operating, the place was to be destroyed. This was to ensure that no one could continue afterwards and sully the family name by selling an inferior tasting product. This lady took her barbecue seriously.

Myrtle Johnson passed away in 1999 at the age of 96 and as far as anyone knows, she took her secret barbecue sauce recipe along with her as she walked through the pearly gates. It's my guess that she is still mixing it up in small batches for St. Peter and the rest of the gang. Those guys know good sauce when they taste it.

In Praise of Ornery Pitmasters
Steven Raichlen really gets it: "One of the things I like best about barbecue is its spirit of individuality—the fact that in our homogenized age, with a fast food outlet on every street corner, barbecue remains some of the last truly regional food in America. I love the fact that barbecue means something different in Lexington, North Carolina, than it does in Lubbock, Texas, or Owensboro, Kentucky. That there are still pitmasters independent (or ornery) enough to stake their reputations on dry rubs versus wet rubs (or vice versa), on hickory versus oak, on spare ribs versus baby backs, and so on."

On The Prowl for BBQ
So let's say you're in a strange town, perhaps on business or on vacation and you develop a strong desire for a pulled pork sammie or a half rack of ribs. Where do you go? What do you do? If you pay attention to the television commercials and technology mavens of today, you should ask your car or your smartphone, "Where's the nearest barbecue restaurant?" Some robotic voice will not only tell you the name and address of the closest 'cue joint, but will also give you directions on how to get there. Wonderful.

Of course, you could Google the question, cruise around the Net to peruse some of the many restaurant rating sites or check out a forum or two. *Blah, blah, blah*, such a bunch of techno babble. But here's a novel idea: you could just ask somebody! I know, I know, very prehistoric and backwards by today's standards, but that's just me. I suggest asking a cop or a firefighter, a local truck driver, the mailperson (notice the politically correct, non-gender specific job titles), or the clerk in the hotel where you are staying. Ask first if they eat barbecue regularly, and if so, where do THEY

Totally Q

go? This is how you find a joint, especially in a tourist area. You want the real skinny on where the locals go to get their regular 'cue fix, not the over-advertised place where all the tourists go because they THINK it's the best.

Once you have a recommendation, you're halfway there. What follows are a few suggestions I have for things to consider BEFORE placing your order:

Photo by Ray Lampe, courtesy of Sunbelt Archives.

• Does the word *barbecue* or any of its derivatives appear in the establishment's name?

• Is there smoke coming from any stacks or chimneys? The absence of smoke is not an automatic deal killer, but should put you on alert.

• Look closely: Do you see any outdoor smokers or cookers? Is there a smoking unit or pit inside the place? Are there any stacks of firewood or bags of charcoal piled about?

• Look at the parking lot.—Do you see a sheriff's car or police cruiser? Is there a combination of work trucks, a few luxury cars, a smattering of SUVs and even a couple of motorcycles? That's a good mix.

• When you walk in the front door, can you smell evidence of recent fires or smoked meat? As anyone who has ever cooked barbecue can attest, the smell of residual smoke can linger for days, and if the smoke is produced on a regular basis, the smell never leaves.

• Is the joint jumping? Any barbecue joint worth its weight in sliced brisket is going to have a steady stream of customers.

• Are there napkin dispensers on each table?

• Who are the customers? Is there a decent mixture of young and old, working class and professional people? Good 'cue draws them all.

• Do they sell fresh-brewed iced tea?

• Are the walls adorned with barbecue memorabilia and photos of folks who have eaten there?

151

Totally Q

- You want the place to be clean, but not sterile; this is a barbecue joint, not an operating room. Look in the restroom—do they have one of those sheets hanging on the door that has to be initialed each time the room is cleaned? If so, is it up to date, or is the last entry from two years ago? This is a tough one, and can go either way. I've found that it's best to base your decision on whether there is a sheet at all, as the date of entries don't carry enough weight on their own to make or break a deal.

- Are barbecued items featured prominently in the menu selections? Are the sides along the lines of beans, slaw, hushpuppies and Mac and cheese? This is a big one. If the restaurant's main course offerings consist of items like chicken á la Kiev or macadamia crusted mahi-mahi, perhaps this isn't the place to order ribs or pulled pork, especially if the barbecued items are treated like a sideshow or menu filler. Chances are if you're foolish enough to order 'cue at a place like this, you will get just what you deserve: a microwaved afterthought.

- This last tip is probably the most important bit of advice I can offer for selecting an out-of-town barbecue joint: If you see the word quiche anywhere on the menu, collect your family and run, don't walk walk don't run to the nearest exit. Do not, I repeat, DO NOT even look back.

Flying High for BBQ!

Folks on the border between North and South Carolina have a one-of-a-kind restaurant that is on the radar of barbecue lovers everywhere. located in Bennetsville, South Carolina on Highway 79 East, Stanton's Barbecue Fly-In Restaurant has a 2,300-foot turf runway located directly across the street, making this joint a destination for pilots and drivers alike. On their website at www.stantonsbarbeque.com, the owners boast the fact that many aviators and military personnel take advantage of the runway to drop in for a meal when flying through the area. To further accommodate their air-based clientele, the restaurant hosts a large fly-in each November and additionally broadcasts "Stanton's Barbecue Traffic" on aircraft radio 122.9, presumably so that pilots can place their orders before they land. More conventional travelers need not worry though, because there is also a large parking lot to accommodate those who arrive by land-based vehicles.

Totally Q

Delivering BBQ Coast to Coast

There's a place in Wilson, North Carolina called Bill Ellis Barbecue that has a pretty large area of delivery—the whole country, as a matter of fact. Bill's has a fleet of more than 40 trucks, which includes a number of mobile kitchens and several 18-wheelers used to haul barbecue and catering gear to destinations as far away as Palm Springs, California. In addition, his eat-in restaurant in Wilson, according to local lore, is one of the best around. As a matter of fact, so much pork is used in its day-to-day operations that Bill has decided he would be better off owning and operating his own hog farm.

Burnt Ends

"I tend to distrust any barbecue restaurant that doesn't have sweet tea."
—Fred Thompson

"One of Vince Staten's rules for a good barbecue place is the presence of flies; if there aren't any, you should ask what the flies know that you don't."
—From *Holy Smoke; The Big Book of North Carolina Barbecue* by John Shelton Reed, Dale Volberg Reed and William McKinney

"Wanna know how good a barbecue restaurant is? Take a look at the size of their woodpile." —Big Bob Gibson

"No smoking, we have enough." —A sign displayed over the pit in Miller's Bar-B-Q in San Antonio, Texas

"Waitresses who work the barbecue circuit have a routine. Once you're seated, they take your order within thirty seconds. A minute later they're back with tea, utensils wrapped in a paper napkin, and an apology for keeping you waiting for your meal. Two more minutes pass and your sandwich arrives." —Alan Richardson

"The barbecue business is when you get to charge for doing something you love and would probably be doing anyway." —Big O's Barbecue

"The sounds I associate with barbecue are listening to my brothers chopping barbecue on the chopping block to whatever beat was going through their head at the time and sometimes making up words to fit...You know, they were rapping before rapping was cool." —Johnny Stogner

Totally Q

"We haven't had one fight since we became a barbecue joint." —Steve Connor of Oinkers Family Restaurant in Clayton, Georgia

"Mom was definitely the business side. Dad would have been happy making great barbecue and going broke." —Van Sykes of Bob Sykes Bar-B-Q in Bessemer, Alabama

"Southern barbecue is the closest thing we have in the United States to Europe's wines or cheeses; drive a hundred miles and the barbecue changes."
—John Shelton Reed

"My heart is in barbecue. I was a barbecue man for forty-six years. I can walk into a kitchen, cut a piece of meat, and tell you how long and how fast you cooked it. I know you think I am bullshitting you, but that's the honest truth." —Harry Green

"Ya'll tired of eatin' that barbecue from up the street? Where they give you more sauce than they give you meat? Then bring your big ass down to Bros. Barbecue, 15837 South Crenshaw Boulevard, that's right off Manchester. Bros. Barbecue, tastes so good, make you wanna slap yo' mama! Don't it, Willie?" —Uncle Elroy

A deeelicious BBQ lunch, complete with pulled pork, ribs, and sweet tea. Photo by Rick Browne.

'Cue on the Screen & Tube

Over the years, barbecue, grilling and outdoor cooking have made numerous appearances on television and the big screen. Sometimes it's just a mention or a brief cameo appearance; in other cases, a scene or even an entire film has been built around barbecue.

The Food Network began broadcasting on November 23, 1993, and few will dispute its influence on cooking, food, chefs and cuisine in general. Elevating the term *foodie* to new heights, this network broadcasts a variety of shows about all types of cooking and has created many stars and "in kitchen" personalities who remain influential and active today. The Food Network and other cooking-related cable TV outlets have been a huge factor in the increase of popularity for cooking and food in general, and it's my opinion that the show *BBQ Pitmasters* has been particularly influential in bringing attention not only to competition barbecue, but to all aspects of outdoor cooking.

Indeed, barbecue is now "mainstream," with many folks asserting that it is one of the only true "American" cuisines. During my research, I found references to cookouts or barbecue in many classic and current movies and most every popular sitcom. Heck, I even found 'cue mentioned in the 1939 classic *Gone with the Wind*.

Also, if you have never seen it, you need to Google "Homer Simpson building a barbecue" and watch the 45-second clip on YouTube. The segment is a riot, and accurately portrays the way most males (me included) in America deal with the most dreaded three words a property owner or a wanna-be home improvement contractor can encounter: "Some assembly required." In addition, the clip most assuredly proves that—whether you like it or not, America—barbecue has arrived and is here to stay.

Totally Q

'Cue on the Big Screen

DAVID O. SELZNICK'S ——— MARGARET MITCHELL'S *Story of the Old South*

GONE WITH THE WIND

Gone with the Wind, 1939

In this epic film, the main character Scarlett O'Hara is asked if she will be attending the neighboring Wilkes-Twelve Oaks plantation's barbecue the next day. She answers with one of the several famous lines from this Hollywood classic: "Why, I hadn't thought about that yet. I'll...I'll think about that tomorrow." Additionally, in an attempt to make Ashley Wilkes jealous, Scarlett tells Charles Hamilton, one of the guests, "I want to eat barbecue with you." In all, the word "barbecue" is mentioned eleven times.

Ferris Bueller's Day Off, 1986

Ferris introduces himself as Abe Froman, the "Sausage King" of Chicago. And what are sausages for, if not the grill?

Goodfellas, 1990

Aside from the scenes depicting pasta making/garlic slicing in prison or Henry's gravy making prowess while he thinks he is being chased by helicopters, who can forget the backyard grilling done by Paulie Cicero, the movie's capo?

Fried Green Tomatoes, 1991

Here's a barbecue you definitely would not want to attend. In this movie, Ruth's abusive husband is whacked by Big George and Idgie, then seasoned, salted and peppered, grilled and served to the very detective assigned to investigate his missing person report. As the copper is heaping on praise about how great the meal is, Big George replies: "Thank you, suh. I'd have to say the secret's in the sauce."

Doc Hollywood, 1991

Dr. Benjamin Stone is given a pig in lieu of payment for treating a man's infected toe. The pig is then named Jasmine, and at one point nearly ends up at the butcher's. Whether she eventually meets her maker over a bed of glowing coals is a topic for the sequel.

Primary Colors, 1998

John Travolta plays a former Governor of Arkansas who is running for the White House in this story that pairs up barbecue and politics quite nicely. Does that remind you of anything in our history?

Totally Q

Varsity Blues, 1999
Lineman Billy Bob had a pet pig named Bacon. While receiving nowhere near the face time of one of his most famous predecessors, Arnold Ziffel on *Green Acres*, Bacon was present in a few scenes and certainly deserves mention.

The Cookout, 2004
This is a very funny movie about a recently-signed basketball star who buys a new home in an upscale neighborhood. To celebrate his newfound wealth, Todd Anderson (Quran Pender) plans a family cookout in the backyard shortly after moving in and his family, old friends and neighbors all decide to show up. That's when the fun begins. If you buy the DVD, you also receive some tips on how to throw a good cookout, in addition to some recipes provided by the movie's cast and crew.

Baptists at Our Barbecue, 2004
The citizens of a divided town have a great idea for overcoming their differences: a community barbecue. This comedy shows what can happen when folks get into the blue smoke, oftentimes resulting in things working out for the best.

Gran Torino, 2008
In classic Eastwood style, the main character Walt Kowalski is invited to a cookout by his Hmong neighbors who want to thank him for running off a couple of troublemakers. While sampling traditional delicacies in their home, Walt, ever the international diplomat, snidely remarks, "Just keep your hands off my dog." Rather than becoming offended, the teenage Sue Loi puts him in his place when she shoots back, "No worries, we only eat cats." *Touché.*

Television Programs Starring BBQ

...And They Don't Allow No Squealing About Customer Service
Satriale's Pork Store is a fictional establishment on the HBO series *The Sopranos*. As told in the television show, the pork store was taken over by Johnny Boy Soprano during the 1970s when Francis Satriale failed to make payments on a gambling debt and later committed suicide. The establishment became a frequent backdrop in the show as a regular hangout for both the Gualtieris and the Sopranos.

Luuuuuuuucy!
Lucy needs to get her vacationing husband Ricky out of her hair so she can do her housework. She and Ethel solve the problem by putting their husbands to work building a barbecue in the *I Love Lucy* episode titled "Building a B.B.Q.," Season 6, Episode 23, which originally aired on April 8, 1957.

Totally Q

"...And here's the cookout where you and the Beaver burned the house down!"

Ward Cleaver: Grilling Trendsetter

Ward Cleaver (Hugh Beaumont) was a household name from 1957-1963 as he gave the entire nation an example of what a "real father" was supposed to be like. Unfortunately, most of the audience for the now-famous *Leave it to Beaver* show had fathers who operated in a much different world than did Ward and June. I believe that one of the most significant contributions made by Ward was the way he demonstrated to the entire TV-watching world that it was okay to "barbecue" out back wearing an apron over a stiff starched shirt with necktie and a pair of pressed gabardine slacks. He is found manning the grill in several episodes, cooking dinner for the family's dear friends the Rutherfords (Lumpy's parents), and to this day, there are many times when, in deference to Ward, I, too, don a necktie and slacks to grill up a few steaks for the neighbors.

Leave the Thinking to Beaver:

[*June has prepared a lovely dinner of barbecued pork ribs*]

Ward Cleaver: "Well, you boys are very quiet tonight. What are you thinking about?"

Theodore "Beaver" Cleaver: "I was just thinkin' what I'd do if I was a pig eatin' peoples' ribs."

June Cleaver: "Beaver, please." —From the 1957 series *Leave it to Beaver*

Bill Gannon's Secret Sauce

In an episode of the 1960s cop show *Dragnet* titled "The Big High," Sergeant Joe Friday (Jack Webb) and Officer Bill Gannon (Harry Morgan) are tasked with trying to convince some hip suburbanites that it's a "bad scene" to smoke weed in their home. In typical 60s style, Friday stiffly walks and talks his way through some classic lines that have given this particular episode a cult following similar to that of the movie *Reefer Madness*.

Totally Q

What is less commonly known about this episode happens in the opening five minutes as Officer Gannon sits at his desk with a wide assortment of ingredients laid out before him. When Friday asks what he is doing, he replies , "Barbecue, Joe, it's for the barbecue." Joe replies in typical Friday fashion, "Barbecue sauce?" To which Gannon says, "You say that like it came out of a bottle, Joe. People have been trying to wrangle this recipe out of me for years."

"Did you, or did you not attempt to STEAL my BBQ sauce recipe???"

Friday makes a remark about how much the stuff must have cost when Gannon quips, "These things aren't terribly expensive Joe—it's how you put them together. But you wouldn't understand—you're a bachelor." Gannon goes on to explain that if he ever put his sauce on the market, he could retire on the royalties. "Is that so?" Joe dryly replies.

Toward the end of the scene, Bill swears Joe to secrecy before he reveals the most confidential ingredient of his sauce, the recipe for which he claims he got from an old chef he once knew. "One quart, vanilla ice cream," Gannon deadpans.

Bill invites Joe out to his house that weekend for a barbecue, but Joe declines because he has a date. "We're having lamb, and that's what is great about this sauce—you put it on lamb and you never know it's lamb," Gannon says proudly. I'm not sure how it was back then, but when lamb chops cost over $25 a pound as they do today, I want to taste the lamb, not cover it up.

That's One Clever Porker
Arguably setting the bar for all swine actors going forward, Arnold Ziffel from the sitcom *Green Acres* (1965-1971), was one of the most famous pigs of his time—next to Porky Pig, of course. Arnold was reportedly of American Yorkshire lineage and

159

Totally Q

it's rumored to this day that many livestock artificial insemination firms command a higher price for samples that descended from his loins. Treated like a son by his TV parents Fred and Doris Ziffel, Arnold carried his own lunchbox, had a paper route and was known to be a very good artist. This ability earned him the handle "Porky Picasso," although some of his most abstract works were, at times, misunderstood.

Hawkeye Forgets the Side
Season 3, Episode 11 of the popular TV sitcom M*A*S*H aired for the first time on November 26, 1974. Titled "Adam's Ribs," it depicted a situation in which Hawkeye Pierce was so fed up with Army food that he had a friend ship him 10 pounds of spareribs and a pint and a half of sauce from Adam's Ribs in Chicago. The joint was fictional, according to Larry Gelbart, one of the show's producers, who explained that the name and location were meant to pay homage to the city's reputation as the "hog butchering capital of the world."After going through a lot of trouble to get the coveted ribs ordered, picked up and shipped, Pierce was still not a happy camper. Why, you ask? Because he forgot to order the coleslaw!

Blood is Thicker Than Sauce
Blood and Sauce is the 204th episode of King of the Hill, the animated series starring propane salesman extraordinaire Hank Hill. In this installment, Hank's son Bobby agrees to assist Bill, a neighbor, with the preparation of his family's secret barbecue sauce. The sauce is a big hit when slathered onto a few ribs, especially when Hank takes a rack or two into work for the guys at the plant.

Homer Simpson on Grilling, as Reported in Parade Magazine
1) To make grilled food taste terrific, my secret ingredient is beer: Add 72 ounces to stomach, then cook. I also find that a half pound of meat really wakes up a veggie burger.
2) To keep the bugs from biting, I move everything indoors and barbecue in the house. It also makes the kids nice and sleepy.

3) I keep kabob skewers handy for unwanted guests, like my annoying neighbor Ned Flanders. And I don't use them for the kabobs.

4) Grill up some vegetables for the vegetarians in your life, like my daughter, Lisa. It's easy. But remember, no matter how you do it, veggies taste bad.

5) Give your backyard get-together a theme. The guests will love it. My favorites

Totally Q

have been the "Quadruple Bypass Anniversary Party" and "The Great Flanders Smoke-Out."

6) What's the best thing to do with leftovers? Leftovers? I never heard of them.

The Cosby Show: "The Barbecue"
Doctor Huxtable shows off his sauce making and grilling skills in Episode 3 of Season 7, which first aired on October 4, 1990. The story involves some of the typical squabbles and drama seen in many of the show's story lines, but in the end, everything is worked out, as usual. The best part, however, is that Doctor H gives all the credit for incident resolution to his special barbecue sauce. Don't we all wish that could really work?

Roseanne: "Scenes from a Barbecue"
This episode portrays the entire clan eating, drinking and singing at the Conners' backyard cookout on Mother's Day. Roseanne was the most-watched show on television between 1989 and 1990, and one of Nielsons' top five rated shows for its first six seasons. "Scenes from a Barbecue" aired on May 7, 1991 and guest-starred Shelley Winters.

The Simpsons: "Lisa the Vegetarian"
In this episode, Lisa visits a petting zoo where she befriends a small lamb, and later comes home to—what else—lamb chops for dinner. As Lisa considers becoming a vegetarian over the injustice, Homer and Bart make fun of her while planning a barbecue—complete with a roasted pig—and even go so far as to form a conga line and chant, "You don't win friends with salad." Lisa ultimately "pignaps" the cooked hog and shoves it off a cliff, giving new meaning to the phrase, "When pigs fly." It first aired on October 15, 1995.

Lisa's Beliefs
Lisa: "I still stand by my beliefs. But I can't defend what I did. I'm sorry I messed up your barbecue."
Homer: "I understand, honey. I used to believe in things when I was a kid."
—From The Simpsons, "Lisa the Vegetarian," 1995

Seinfeld Slaughterhouse
Jerry: "What is this?"
Kramer: "We're making sausages."
Jerry: "I thought you were gonna watch a video."
Kramer: "Yeah, an instructional video about how to make your own sausages."
Jerry: "Kramer, I'm not in the mood for this."

Totally Q

Kramer: "All right, all right. Newman, let's go grab some mail sacks and haul these beauties out of here."
Jerry: "Blood over there, sausages over here. I'm living in a slaughterhouse."
—From *Seinfeld*, "The Blood," 1997

Tony Dons Shorts on *The Sopranos*
Carmine Lupertazzi: "One other thing, though. John told me he went to a cookout at your house."
Tony Soprano: "Yeah."
Carmine Lupertazzi: "A don doesn't wear shorts." —From *The Sopranos*, "For All Debts Public and Private," 2002

King of the Hill: "The Star Game"
Hank (poking the steak while testing for doneness): "Firm but with a little give. Yep, these are medium rare."
Bobby: "What if somebody wants theirs well-done?"
Hank: "We ask them politely but firmly to leave. With great meat, son, comes great responsibility." —From Season 12, 2008

To Sirloin with Love
During the thirteenth season of *King of the Hill*, Hank discovers that Bobby has a previously unknown talent for inspecting, distinguishing and grading cuts of meat. Bobby joins the meat inspection team at Heimlich County Community College and the end of the story finds Hank and Bobby lighting their grills to cook for the neighbors.

Cougars Can't Keep a Secret
Even the new shows want to get in on the act. In a 2009 *Cougar Town* episode called "Don't Come Around Here No More," the entire cast shows up at what was supposed to be a secret barbecue thrown by Jules.

Burning Up in Suburgatory
In a 2011 *Suburgatory* episode titled "The Barbecue," George learns that as the newest neighbor to the community of Chatswin, he has to host the neighborhood barbecue or risk being ostracized. I have to admit that after watching this show once or twice with my wife, I think I'd rather be ostracized than spend my time with this wacky bunch of overinflated misfits.

No Shit, It's Norm!
Journalist Jeffery Steingarten wrote an article in the September 1992 issue of *Vogue* magazine all about the Memphis in May Barbecue Cooking Contest where the

Totally Q

overall Grand Champion that year was none other than Apple City Barbecue. This team from Murphysboro, Illinois was led by Mike Mills, the owner of the 17th Street Bar and Grill, which is located in downtown Murphysboro.

Early one morning, Mike received an order for his ribs from a caller who identified himself as George Wendt. Mike was busy at the time smoking ribs for a big vending gig he had on the calendar, so he told the guy to call back. The caller then said, "Let me give you my name again. This is George Wendt, I am Norm on Cheers." "No shit?" replied Mike. "Yeah, no shit," George replied. Wendt got his ribs and became one of Mills' many loyal customers.

Reality BBQ TV

Food on TV?
"Who in the world would want to watch cooking shows all day long?" The answer, of course, was: Millions of people.

Barbecue University and *Primal Grill*
Featuring Steven Raichlen, author of numerous barbecue books, including *BBQ USA* and *Planet Barbecue*, these shows are great for learning techniques and procedures and provide a valuable resource for new recipes. First airing on PBS, some of the episodes are now available on DVD.

BBQ TV
BBQ TV is an Internet broadcasting site that contains a ton of good information. You can find contest updates, cooking demonstrations, video recipes, stories on barbecue joints, and much more. It's all there for the viewing, anytime you want it. Sort of a "barbecue on demand."

Grillin' and Chillin'
Grillin' and Chillin' made its network debut on The Food Network in 1995, featuring Bobby Flay and Jack McDavid. Some say it was the first program to bring barbecue and outdoor cooking to television on a regular basis.

The BBQ Championship Series on Versus
This 2006 television show filmed in Reno, Nevada highlighted some of barbecue's heavy hitters including Mike Davis, Johnny Trigg, Myron Mixon, Ray Lampe, Jack McDavid, Byron Chism and Adam Perry Lang, just to name a few. The show aired on the Versus Network, was sponsored by Kingsford Charcoal and featured Darryl Dawkins as one of the judges.

163

Totally Q

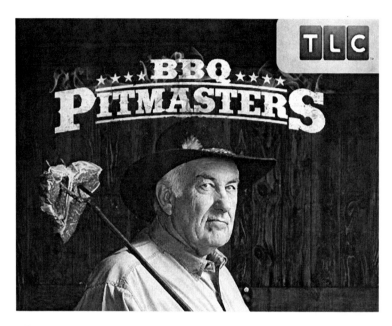

BBQ Pitmasters

What is considered by many competition cooks to be the best and most appealing format of all the reality barbecue shows, BBQ Pitmasters follows barbecue cooks as they competed for cash and prizes. Season 1 began in 2009 and was filmed on location at several barbecue contests around the country. Season 2 unfolded in a stationary location and featured the drama as last-minute categories were tossed at the pitmasters to confound them and ramp up the excitement. It seems the jury is still out as to whether this was effective.

After Season 2, the show moved from the TLC network to Destination America, which announced in June 2012, that the third season of BBQ Pitmasters set viewer records. "Barbecue Pitmasters is Destination America's #1 original series ever, among all key demographics," they said in a press release. And there's plenty more where that came from. You can bet that the show's producer John Markus, who is also a competition barbecue cook and outdoor cooking aficionado, will continue to work very hard to bring the very best barbecue to your home TV screen. Sometimes when I watch the reruns, I swear I can smell smoke.

The Ultimate BBQ Showdown

Memorial Day weekend 2011 marked the first time a major television network (CBS) had ever aired a competition barbecue show. The prime time format featured four top

Totally Q

barbecue cooks: Myron Mixon, Tuffy Stone, Neil "Big Mista" Stawder, and Bubba Latimer, who duked it out in a winner-take-all battle for prizes that , included the Kingsford Cup, some cash, and a whole lot of bragging rights. Notable personalities included Judges Chris Lilly, Ray Lampe, and Mike Lake, as well as Producer John Markus of *BBQ Pitmasters* fame.

Best in Smoke
This Food Network production, set in a park just outside New York City, first aired in May of 2011. In the show, six pitmasters from around the country, including Chris Hart, "Famous Dave" Anderson, Matt Lang, Sara Horowitz, Chris Lilly and Brad Orrison, competed in a series of challenging tasks for a top prize of $50,000.

Chopped Barbecue
No, I'm not talking about chopped pork shoulder here. I'm referring to the TV show *Chopped*, another Food Network production that has become very popular. This is a show where three judges (I know...yawn...we haven't seen this concept anywhere before) taste the submissions of three or four cooks and then decide who stays and who gets "chopped." Get it? To be honest, it's a pretty good show. In the summer of 2012, *Chopped* got aboard the barbecue train with a five-week series that tested the mettle of some of the country's premier grill-meisters, all of whom were competing for $50,000 in prize money.

Burnt Ends

"A couple of pip pips, a little barbecue, and what have you!" —Shemp Howard from the 1949 *Three Stooges* episode, "Who Done It?"

"Ok, everyone's invited to my place in Bel Air for a buffalo barbecue!"—Moe Howard after the filming of the 1965 Three Stooges movie, *The Outlaws IS Coming*

"When we get to Largo, you can have the mayor's horse, fried or barbecued." —Stacey Bridges, an outlaw from *High Plains Drifter*, 1973

"I'm gonna barbecue yo' ass in molasses!" —Sheriff Buford T. Justice from *Smokey and the Bandit*, 1977

"You know what the gourmet here wanted? Hot dogs! You know what they're made of, Chet? Huh? Lips and assholes!"—Roman while barbecuing lobsters in *The Great Outdoors*, 1988

Totally Q

"Umm... you're a really good barbecue...tionist." —Seth Cohen from the debut episode of *The OC*, 2003

"I will say one thing for her, Ed. She does have a nice big 'ole behind. I'd like to put some barbecue sauce on that butt ..." —The Champ, from the 2004 film *Anchorman: The Legend of Ron Burgundy*

"Ah...look at Hank Hill concentrate—his mind a total blank, he's in a state of redneck transcendence." —A neighbor's comment from *King of the Hill*, made while watching Hank grill some steaks

"Le Grill? What the hell is that?!!"—Homer Simpson

"Yeah...that's one fine looking barbecue pit." (then, surveying the results of all of his labors): "WHY DOESN'T MINE LOOK LIKE THAT?!!" —Homer Simpson, while looking at the picture on the cover of a barbecue cooker kit in *The Simpsons*

"Peggy, you're not going to believe this—I was naked, I was grilling burgers naked. How do you like that?" — Hank Hill from *King of the Hill*, describing a dream to his wife

The 'Cue-iz: Test Your BBQ Knowledge

I guess by now, you have picked up on the fact that I have once again evoked literary license with the ever-so-corny take on the word quiz. As much as I know you hate pop quizzes, (doesn't everybody?) I encourage you to take this one. Rest assured no one from the control group bombed completely, but I guess in the interest of full disclosure, I should also tell you that the control group was made up of nothing but a bunch of half drunk, slightly past middle-age, portly, usually sauce-stained, wannabe barbecue rejects. Not exactly MENSA material. Wait a minute—I think I just described myself and some of my friends (certainly not with the MENSA mention).

So with all that in mind, let us begin. The instructions are the same as when you were in school: Select THE BEST answer.

1. The Big High episode of the 1960s television show Dragnet has developed a sort of cult following for several reasons. Of interest here, is the revelation of Bill Gannon's well-kept recipe for his homemade barbecue sauce. What was his most secret ingredient?

a) Cannabis

b) A 12-ounce can of root beer

c) One quart of vanilla ice cream

d) A sliced hardboiled egg

2. True or False: Barbecue is a noun, a verb, and an adjective.

3. In 1936, President and Mrs. Roosevelt served hot dogs to the king and queen of England for what reason?

a) The Royals arrived unannounced and when Mrs. R. went to the fridge, the only thing she found were some hot dogs, a few slices of three-day-old pizza and a couple

Totally Q

of cartons of leftover Chinese food.

b) The Roosevelts weren't concerned about opinion polls or political correctness and thought a simple dinner of tube steaks would be something the king and queen would enjoy.

c) The president knew he would make the Republicans mad by serving hot dogs in the White House, particularly if they were processed and manufactured by union meat cutters.

d) The king and queen had fallen in love with American hot dogs after a short visit just days earlier to Coney Island.

4. The discovery of fire over 400,000 years ago was very important to barbecuing for what reason?

a) Without fire, man would be eating brisket uncooked—and raw brisket is extremely tough and hard to chew.

b) Fire enabled man to discover fine cigars, thus creating a huge black market for cigar manufacturers from Cuba here in the United States.

c) The discovery of fire led to the creation of fire companies, which ultimately led to the brightly colored fire trucks that are integral in towns across America for leading Fourth of July parades.

d) Fire, from a multitude of different sources, plays a very important part in grilling, smoking, barbecuing or any type of outdoor cooking.

5. True or False: Harry Soo and his Slap Yo' Daddy BBQ competition barbecue team have been one of the only teams in a KCBS-sanctioned contest to take first place in all four categories.

6. The reason Fred Flintstone's car tipped over when the waitress placed a large slab of ribs on the serving tray was:

a) Fred had already been served a brontosaurus burger and the combined weight was too much.

b) The car really didn't flip over—it was all done with special effects.

c) Barney rigged the car to roll over as payback for Fred not returning the lawnmower he had borrowed a month earlier.

d) I have no idea.

7. What fuel source was used for the urn-shaped cooking device that dated back to 2600 B.C. and was found by explorers?

168

Totally Q

a) Pellets

b) Gas

c) Lump charcoal

d) Charcoal briquettes

e) I don't really care.

8. In what year did "Fast Eddie" Maurin first manufacture his pellet cookers?

a) 1990

b) 1994

c) 1996

d) 1999

9. In the 1974 episode of M*A*S*H titled *Adam's Ribs*, what did Hawkeye Pierce forget to order during his long-distance takeout call?

a) Coleslaw

a) Napkins

b) Hushpuppies

c) Cheer soda

10. Who of the following IS already a member of the Barbecue Hall of Fame?

a) Speed Herrig

b) Dave Thomas

c) Al Gore

d) Ronald McDonald

11. Porky Pig's father went by the name of:

a) Phineas

b) Poindexter

c) Arnold

d) Percival

12. The KCBS *Bullsheet* is published:

a) Once in a while

Totally Q

b) Weekly

c) Monthly

d) Bimonthly

13. In 1916, the very first Nathan's Famous Fourth of July Hot Dog Eating Contest on Coney Island, New York was won by:

a) Jason Schecter

b) James Mullen

c) Joey Chestnut

d) Takeru Kobayashi

14. Who wished he would have said, "We will sell no swine before its time?"

a) Paul Masson

b) Joey Chestnut (again?)

c) Porky Pig

d) Arnold Ziffel

15. Que- Eau De Barbeque is:

a) A barbecue cologne

b) The aroma emitting from your T-shirt after a long day on the grill

c) French for "pass me the barbecue sauce"

d) All of the above

16. Jasper the pig is famous for what?

a) Working as a stand-in for Porky Pig in many of the later cartoons, especially after Porky developed his well known drinking habit

b) Winning *American Idol*, Season 4

c) Nothing at all

d) Being the vessel in which barbecuers from around the country burn their written regrets each year at the Jack Daniel's World Championship Invitational Barbecue

17. In the 2008 movie *Gran Torino*, Clint Eastwood's gruff character Walt Kowalski is invited to a cookout at the neighbor's house. The hosts are Hmong, and as Walt is

pokes around the *hors d'oeuvre* platter, he crudely cracks, "Just keep your hands off my dog." Sue Loi, the teenage girl who lives in the house, shoots back a catty remark of her own when she replies:

a) "No worries, we only eat cat."

b) "We don't like dog unless it is slow smoked, and then it is hard to keep lit."

c) "Dogs, we don't need no stinkin' dogs."

d) "This wasn't your dog."

18. After being denied a second term in 1962, Georgia Governor Marvin Griffins was heard to make which of the following statements?

a) "Some of the people who ate my barbecue didn't vote for me."

b) "I am not a crook."

c) "Read my lips; no new taxes."

d) "We have to pass the bill to find out what is in it."

19. The North American Chapter of WTHDBBQMTM exists where?

a) In South America

b) In the northern part of the country

c) In the author's warped and demented imagination

d) None of the above

20. True or False: Microsoft Word, one of the most popular word processing programs, allows for two correct spellings of the word barbeque/barbecue.

21. According to *Sound Suds Advice*, when it comes to beer and barbecue, what is the cardinal rule?

a) Always drink the host's beer first

b) Never bring your own beer to a barbecue

c) Upon arrival, bypass the champagne cocktails and head straight for the brew

d) Drink only water at all outdoor functions; it is much better for your overall hydration

22. President Dwight Eisenhower was famous for which of the following?

a) Working as a movie star before entering the world of politics

Totally Q

b) Grilling his steaks right on the charcoal

c) Explaining to the nation the definition of the word "is"

d) Cooking out on the roof of the White House

e) Both (b) and (d)

23. If you are flying your plane in the area near Bennetsville, South Carolina and you develop a hankering for a pulled pork platter, the best thing you can do is:

a) Proceed to your destination and deal with the urge at the barbecue joint of your choice.

b) Return to your airport of origin immediately. Flying while hungry, especially for barbecue, can be very distracting. Once on the ground, fill the void with something from the airpark vending machines, which ought to hold you over or send you running to the can. Either way, you'll forget about barbecue for a while.

c) Locate the coordinates for Stanton's Barbecue Fly-In Restaurant, located on the border between North and South Carolina. You can also attempt to raise Stanton's BBQ Traffic on your plane's radio as they do monitor the channel and accept phone-in orders.

d) Ask the co-pilot or other passengers to check all seat pouches, jacket pockets, carry-ons, pocketbooks, etc. for any and all available candy bars, granola bars, jerky sticks or other edible rations. If you have direct knowledge of fast food ever having been consumed in the cockpit area, be sure to have someone check underneath and on the sides of all seats for stray French fries.

24. At a cookout or barbecue, the male of the species will always gather around the grill or smoker. The question is: Why?

a) They know they will be left alone because females do not like smoke.

b) The cooker is usually near the cooler, hence, the location is a win-win.

c) They can't help themselves, the combination of burning meat and aromatic smoke is too much to resist.

d) Other males will be present and they are by nature herd mammals.

e) They huddle here in hopes of gathering pearls of wisdom regarding various types of outdoor cookery.

25. Which of the following is *not* a name for a type of cloud?

a) Cirrostratus

Totally Q

b) Cirrus

c) Cumulus

d) Lump charcoal

The Answers

1. c

2. True

3. While there are a few possibilities here, the correct answer is "b."

4. d

5. True

6. d

7. c —I know, this answer is not in the text, I just made it up.

8. b

9. a

10. a

11. a —If you got this one right, you're pretty good, the answer wasn't even in the book.

12. c

13. b

14. a

15. a

16. d

17. a

18. a

19. c

20. True

21. While one might be tempted to select either "a"or "b," the correct answer from the text is "c." Why anyone in the world would want to attend an outdoor function and drink only water is beyond me. If that's the case, they might just as well stay home.

22. e

23. c —Of course this is the best and correct answer. However, in a weak moment, I may accept "a." If you picked "b" or "d," I think you are goofier than I am.

24. Again, any answer will be acceptable here. (I know, I'm making this too easy for you, but I know after all these questions, I have a real chance of losing your interest, so I'm doing my best to keep you entertained)

25. That's right, "d." I hope you got this one right, as I am running out of material.

Totally Q

Appendix

Wherein I share all the other information that's not particularly funny, but very useful.

Some Favorite Barbecue Books:

Big Time Barbecue by Ray Lampe, AKA Dr. BBQ

Peace, Love and Barbecue by Mike and Amy Mills

Smokin' by Myron Mixon

Big Bob Gibson's BBQ Book by Chris Lilly

Wicked Good Barbecue by Andy Husbands and Chris Hart

Char-Broil America Grills by Creative Homeowner

Mastering Barbecue by Michael Stines

The Kansas City Barbecue Society Cookbook by Ardie Davis, Paul Kirk, and Carolyn Wells

Favorite Barbecue Forums:

The BBQ Brethren, http://www.bbq-brethren.com/forum/

The BBQ Forum, http://www.rbjb.com/rbjb/rbjbboard/

Favorite barbecue websites, blogs, etc:

Diva Q, http://divaq.ca/

Amazing Ribs, http://www.amazingribs.com/

The BBQ Grail, http://thebbqgrail.com/

The BBQ Smoker Site, http://www.bbqsmokersite.com/

Fat Johnny's Front Porch, http://chez-frontporch.blogspot.com/

Sources for Sauces, Rubs, and Other Assorted Good Stuff:

Hawgeyes BBQ, http://www.hawgeyesbbq.com/

3 Eyz BBQ, http://www.3eyzbbq.com/

New England BBQ and Catering, http://www.bbqnewengland.com/

The BBQ Guru, http://www.thebbqguru.com/

The Ingredient Store, http://www.theingredientstore.com/

Dizzy Pig Barbecue Company, http://www.dizzypigbbq.com/

Totally Q

Memphis In May Grand Champions, With Winning Category

1978	Bessie Lou Cathey	Ribs
1979	Don Burdison	Ribs
1980	John Wills	Ribs
1981	John Wills	Ribs
1982	Martec Coaters	Shoulders
1983	Willingham's River City Rooters	Ribs
1984	Willingham's River City Rooters	Ribs
1985	Holy Smokers, Too	Whole Hog
1986	Pig Iron Porkers	Whole Hog
1987	Cajun County Cookers	Whole Hog
1988	Holy Smokers, Too	Whole Hog
1989	Super Swine Sizzlers	Whole Hog
1990	Apple City Barbecue	Ribs
1991	David Cox Barbecue Team	Ribs
1992	Apple City Barbecue	Ribs
1993	The Other Side	Shoulders
1994	Apple City Barbecue	Ribs
1995	Rebel Roaster Revue	Shoulders
1996	Pyropigmaniacs	Ribs
1997	Wildfire Gourmet Cooking Team	Shoulders
1998	The Other Team	Ribs
1999	Custom Cookers	Whole Hog
2000	Big Bob Gibson	Shoulders
2001	Jack's Old South	Whole Hog
2002	Pyropigmaniacs	Ribs
2003	Big Bob Gibson	Shoulders
2004	Jack's Old South	Whole Hog
2005	Gwatney	Whole Hog
2006	Red Hot Smokers	Shoulders
2007	Jack's Old South	Whole Hog
2008	Natural Born Grillers	Whole Hog
2009	Sweet Swine O Mine	Shoulders
2010	Yazoo Delta Q	Whole Hog
2011	Big Bob Gibson	Shoulders
2012	Yazoo Delta Q	Whole Hog
2013	Sweet Swine O' Mine	Shoulders

Totally Q

The American Royal World Series of Barbecue © Winners

YEAR	OPEN GRAND CHAMPION	INVITATIONAL GRAND CHAMPION
1987	What's A Matta You	
1988	Meadowbrook Country Club	Schroeger Brothers
1989	Campbell Point Burnt Ends	Harley's Fencing Crew
1990	Lone Wolf Cookers	Bad Company BBQ
1991	KC Baron of BBQ	
1992	Hawg Pen	
1993	Slaughterhouse Five	Hoelting Brothers
1994	Heat's Neat	
1995	Special Edition	
1996	Redneck Cookers	
1997	Fat Boys BBQ	3 Little Pigs
1998	Three Little Pigs	USA Smoke
1999	Three Little Pigs	USA Smoke
2000	Pig Newton	3 Little Pigs
2001	Big Red Barbecue	Buttrub.com
2002	Lotta Bull BBQ	Smokin' in the Dark
2003	Grilla's	Four Men and a Pig
2004	Boys From Tornado Alley-	Big Bob Gibson
2005	Lotta Bull BBQ-	Great Grills O Fire
2006	Habitual Smokers	Lotta Bull BBQ
2007	Bubba and Jeff's BBQ	Great Grills O Fire
2008	Four Men And A Pig	Joey Mac's Smoke Stax
2009	Boondoggle BBQ	Pork Pullin Plowboys
2010	Lotta Bull BBQ-	Smokers Wild
2011	Motley Que Crew	Tippycanoe BBQ
2012	Shiggin & Grinnin	Big Poppa Smokers

Totally Q

Jack Daniel's World Championship BBQ Grand Champions

1989	Team Kansas City, KC, MO - Paul Kirk
1990	Super Swine Sizzlers, West Memphis, AR - Jim Turner
1991	Eddy's Catering/Flower of the Flame, Gladstone, MO - Karen Putman
1992	Apple City BBQ, Murphysboro, IL - Mike Mills
1993	Oklahoma Joe's Hogamaniacs, Stillwater, OK - Joe Davidson
1994	Head Country BBQ II, Ponca City, OK - Paul Schatte
1995	Kamikaze Kookers, IN
1996	Pyropigmaniacs, Memphis, TN - Bill Bryant
1997	Smokin' in the Boys Room, Leawood, KS - Richard Kancel
1998	Fat Boys, Temple, TX - Danny Mikes
1999	Smokin' Guns BBQ, Kansas City, MO - Phil Hopkins
2000	Smokin' Triggers, Alvarado, TX - Johnny Trigg
2001	Twin Oak Smokin Crew, Stillwater, OK - Bart Clark
2002	Wee Willy's, Afton, MN - Bill Scanlon
2003	Smokin Triggers, Alvarado, TX - Johnny Trigg
2004	Mad Cow, England - Rick Weight
2005	Boys from Tornado Alley, Sperry/Stillwater, OK - Donny Teal & Bart Clark
2006	Cancersuckschicago.com, Westmont, IL - Scottie Johnson
2007	Moonswiners, Taylorsville, KY - Chad Hayden
2008	Four Leg's Up, Great Bend, KS - Kelly Wertz
2009	I Que, Hopkinton, MA. - Chris Hart
2010	QUAU, Brimfiled, Il - Mike Wozniak
2011	Smokin' Hoggz BBQ- Bill Gillespie
2012	Pig Skin BBQ, Rockwell, IA - Scott Nelson

Totally Q

KCBS Team of the Year By Year
1994-1996 – Happy Holla
1997 – Armadillo Bob's Bar-B-Q
1998 – Smokin' in the Boys Room
1999 – Smokin' in the Boys Room
2000 – Smokin' in the Boys Room
2001 – Smokin' in the Boys Room
2002 – PDT
2003 – Smokin' Triggers
2004 – Twin Oak Smokin Crew
2005 – Twin Oak Smokin Crew
2006 - Lotta Bull BBQ
2007 – Cool Smoke
2008 – Munchin Hogs at the Hilton
2009 – Pellet Envy
2010 – QUAU
2011 – Munchin' Hogs at the Hilton
2012 – 3 Eyz BBQ

Barbecue Abbreviations
ABT- Atomic Buffalo Turd
BBQ- barbecue (did I really have to include this one?)
CBBQA- California Barbecue Association
DAL- Dead assed last- a position to be avoided when competing in a barbecue contest, or any contest for that matter.
FBA- Florida Barbecue Association
FEC- Fast Eddy Cooker
IMBBQA-Intermountian Barbecue Association
KCBS- Kansas City Barbecue Society
MBN- Memphis Barbecue Network
MIM- Memphis in May World Championship Barbecue Cooking Contest
NBBQA- National Barbecue Association
NEBS- New England Barbecue Society
Ph.B.- Doctorate in Barbecue Philosophy form Greasehouse University
UDS- Ugly Drum Smoker
WSM- Weber Smokey Mountain
WTHDBBQMTM- What The Heck Does BBQ Mean To Me

Totally Q

Barbecue's High Holy Days

February 29: National Surf and Turf Day
March 1: National Pig Day
May: National Barbecue Month
May: National Grilling Month
May: National Hamburger Month
May 28: National Hamburger Day and National Brisket Day
July: National Grilling Month
July: National Hot Dog Month
July: National Baked Bean Month
July National Barbecued Spare Ribs Month
July 13: Bean 'N' Franks Day
July 20: National Hot Dog Day
August 11: Feast of Saint Alexander "the charcoal burner"
August 13: National Filet Mignon Month
August 16: National Bratwurst Day
August 19: Hot & Spicy Food Day
August 31: National Eat Outside Day
September: National Chicken Month
October: National Pork Month
December 5: Repeal of Prohibition Day (woo hoo!)

Totally Q

Tunes to BBQ By

A&R BBQ- Steve Smith and the M

A Chicken Ain't Nothin' but a Bird- Nellie Lutcher

A Chicken Can Waltz the Gravy Around- Stovepipe No. 1 & David Crockett

A Georgia Barbecue at Stone Mountain Part 1 – John Dilleshaw

A Quiche Woman in a Barbeque Town- Clyde Edgerton

A Quiet Barbecue- David Gilchrist

Ain't No Barbecue In Heaven- Daddy Bone

Ain't Nobody Here But us Chickens- Louie Jordan

Alabama BBQ- The Ink Spots

All My Rowdy Friends Are Coming Over Tonight- Hank Williams, Jr.

All that meat and no Potatoes- Fats Waller

Alligator Meat- Big Sofa and the Lazy Boys

Andouille- Bill "Sauce Boss" Wharton & the Ingredients

Anybody Here Want to Try My Cabbage?- Fats Waller

Appetite Blues- Lightnin' Hopkins

Auntie Skinner's Chicken Dinner-Bob Hodes Red Onion Jazz Band

Aussie BBQ- The Aussie Bush Band

Backer City BBQ- Jimmy Lloyd Rea and the Switchmasters

Backyard Barbecue- Against the Grain

Backwoods BBQ- Tom Coerver

Bar-B-Q Sauce- Sam Price

Bar-B-Q- Wendy Rene

Barbecue- Alan Greenleaf & The Doctor

Barbecue- Cotton Belly's

Barbecue- Handsome Devil

Barbecue -JoJo Ryder

Barbecue- Muck Sticky

Barbecue- Washboard Sam

Barbecue Any Old Time- Brownie McGhee

Barbecue Anytime- The Alabama Gravy Stoppers

Barbecue Bob in Fishtown- Glenn Jones

Barbecue Boogie- Elvin Bishop

Barbecue at Phil's- Sea Monster

Barbecue Baby- Luther Badman Keith

Barbecue Bess- Lucille Bogan & Bess Jackson

Barbecue Blues- Barbecue Bob

Barbecue Bop- Eddie Martin

Barbecue Bust- Mississippi Jook Band

Barbecue Chicken- Bubblin' Toorop Trio

Totally Q

Barbecue Circle Pit- Lousy (please listen to sample before downloading)
Barbecue Country Style- Brian Callies
Barbecue Down in Georgia Part 2- Hershel Brown
Barbecue Friends- The Fierce Lime and His Ponytail Assassins
Barbecue Girl- Kathryn Scheldt
Barbecue Grill- Amanda and the White Toed Cat
Barbecue in Bhopal-Mumakil (you have got to be kidding)
Barbecue On Broadway- Juggernant Jug Band
Barbecue Party- Koichiro Hara
Barbecue Pleasure- Jimi Tenor
Barbecue Rag- Felix Janosa
Barbecue Rock- Peter Xanten's Ragtime Band
Barbecue Sauce- Mark Stepakoff
Barbecue Shoes- Blue House
Barbecue Swing- Helios Fernandez
Barbecue Steak- Enok
Barbecue, Whiskey, and Blues- Dieter Kropp & The Red Hot Blues Band
Barbecue With Friends- DJ Shah
Barbeque- Buzz Cason
Barbeque- Cross Timbers
Barbeque- Duke Tumatoe
Bar-B-Que- Wendy Rene
Barbeque- Hayseed Dixie
Barbeque- Mumbo Gumbo
Barbeque- Ray Stevens
Barbeque- The Red Clay Ramblers
Barbeque- Robert Earl Keen
Barbeque- The Mission Three
Barbeque and Drink a Few- Travis Matte and the Zydeco Kingpins
Barbeque Joe's- Starline Rhythm Boys
Barbeque King- Jorma Kaukonen
Barbeque On My Birthday- Dawn Sears
Barbeque On My Boogie- Michael Katon
Barbequed Ribs- Three Riffs
Barbecue Shoes- Blue House
Barnyard Banjo Picken- Stringbean
Barnyard Boogie - Louie Jordan
BBQ- Mojo Gumbo
BBQ- Steven Seagal
BBQ- The Dirty Mac Blues Band

Totally Q

BBQ- The Master Plan
BBQ - The Blind Chitlin Kahunas
BBQ at JD's- Rick Holstrom
BBQ at Sadies- Wake Campbell
BBQ Bash- Marc Baril
BBQ Girl- Graveyard BBQ
Bbq Is Mighty Good- Don Morrison
BBQ Nation- Graveyard BBQ
BBQ Party- Shonen Knife
BBQ Police- Soap Star Joe
BBQ Ribs- Tommy Largo
BBQ Roadhouse Blues- The Funkdawgs
BBQ Song - Rhett and Link
BBQ Stain- Tim McGraw
BBQ USA- Mojo Nixon
Beach Barbecue- Super Crunch
Beale Street Bar-B-Q-The Memphis Boys
Beans & Cornbread- Louie Jordan
Bedroom Barbecue- Andy Hollinden
Beer & BBQ's- The Works
Big Balls in Cowtown- Asleep at the Wheel
Big Barbecue- Amy X Newburg & Men
Big Boy Barbecue- Nuts and Bolts
Big Fat Ham-Jelly Roll Morton
Bill's Laundromat Bar And Grill- Confederate Railroad
Billy's Bayou Barroom & Backyard Barbecue- Michael McCloud
Black Coffee- Billy Holliday
Bless This Barbeque- Billy O'Rourke
Blessing of the Pork - Billy Ray Mangham
Blind Pig Blues- Barbecue Bob
Blue Eyed Woman- John Primer
Blues, Booze, and Barbecue- Nick Branch
Blues For The Barbecue- Count Bassie
Boogie Woogie Bar-B-Q- Mitch Woods
Brown Chicken, Brown Cow- Trace Adkins
Burger Man - ZZ Top
Catfish and Collard Greens- Junior Brown
Catfish Fry- Red Meat
Cattle Call- Roy Rogers
Cheeseburger in Paradise- Jimmy Buffet

Totally Q

Chicken and Dumplings- Kermit Ruffins and the Barbecue Swingers
Chicken BBQ- Karl Allweier
Chicken Blues- Billy Ward & The Dominoes
Chicken Bop- Truitt Forse
Chicken Cordon Blues- Steve Goodman
Chicken, Gravy and Biscuits- Lil' Ed & The Blues Imperials
Chicken Hearted Women- Clarence Samuels
Chicken Inn The Basket- The Tri-cones
Chicken in the Gumbo- Bill "Sauce Boss" Wharton & the Ingredients
Chicken Rhythm-Slim Gaillard
Chicken Shack Boogie- Bootleg Kings
Chicken Song- Ernest Tubb
Chicken Soup with Rice - Carole King
Chicken Stuff- Hop Wilson
Chili Sauce- Louis Prima
Chittlin' Ball- King Porter
Chittlin Switch Blues- Slim Gaillard
Chocolate Pork Chop Man- Pete 'Guitar' Lewis
Chop That BBQ_ Herman Matthews
Christmas by the Bar-B-Que- Lynn August (This has got to be one of the only barbecue/Christmas songs in existence)
Chucks Barbecue- Some of my Best Friends
Cincinnati Dancing Pig- Red Foley
Cindy Tastes of Barbecue- Luna
Clothing Optional Christian Barbecue- Tennis Pro
Cut the Mustard- Bobby Bare
Come on Down- Jolly Two
Cole Slaw- Jesse Stone
Colonel Josh's BBQ- Asylum Street Spankers
Come On Over to My BBQ-   Laurie Morvan Band
Complimentary Barbeque- The Panfil Brothers
Cooking Big Woman-Guitar Slim
Cool Buds and a Barbecue- Stolen Oregano
Corn Licker & Barbecue Part 2- Fiddlin John Carson
Country BBQ- Steve & Heather
Dancin BBQ? It is a Barbecue Tonight?- Pan
Darktown Barbecue- William Brown
Deans Barbecue- Richie Furay
Diggin my Potatoes- Bill "Sauce Boss" Wharton & the Ingredients
Dinner Bell- They Might Be Giants

184

Totally Q

Dixie Chicken- Little Feat
Dixie Fried - Kentucky Headhunters
Dixie Pig Barbecue- Euphoria
Dixie Rose Deluxe's Honky-Tonk, Feed Store, Gun Shop, Used Car, Beer, Bait, BBQ, Barber Shop, Laundromat- Trent Willmon
Don't Get Behind on Your BBQ- Red Clay Ramblers
Down At Jasper's Bar-B-Que - Frankie 'Half Pint' Jaxon
Drink that Mash and Talk That Trash- Flat & Scruggs
East Carolina Barbecue Blues- Willie Nelms
Eat Your Wife and Kiss the Barbecue- Mount Righteous
Eatin' With The Boogie- Slim Gaillard
Eating Greens - Michael Tilson Thomas
Eggs & Sausage- Tom Waits
Ending Barbecue- Burning Sausages (the artist name alone should keep you from looking this one up)
Everybody's Eatin Barbecue- Pat Costello
Everyone Eats When They Come to My House- Cab Calloway
Every Time I Eat Vegetables It Makes Me Think of You- The Ramones
Fat Meat Is Good Meat- Savannah Churchill and her All Star Seven
Fatback Louisiana, USA- Tennessee Ernie Ford
Feel the Fire...From Barbecue- Massacration (a real head-banger)
Fred's Barbecue House- The Big Ragoo
Fried Bananas - Dexter Gordon
Fried Chicken and Gasoline- Southern Culture on the Skids
Fried Neck Bones and Some Home Fries- Willie Bobo
Frim Fram Sauce- Nat King Cole or Ella Fitzgerald
Fritos, BBQ & Scotch- Paul Mark & the Van Dorens
Frog Barbecue- Uncle Ed's Rocking Rodeo
Front Yard BBQ- Whiskeydick
Gallipolli BBQ- Simply Bushed
Get Your Biscuits In The Oven And Your Buns In Bed- Kinky Friedman
Gimme a Pig's Foot and a Bottle of Beer- Frankie 'Half Pint' Jaxon
Goin' On Down to the BBQ- Stan Ridgway and Drywall
Good BBQ- The Riptones
Good Booty and Barbecue- Out of Favor Boys
Gotta Sell Them Chickens- Hank Thompson
Great Big Fanny- Bill "Sauce Boss" Wharton & the Ingredients
Great Scott's BBQ- R.C. Banks
Grits ain't Groceries- Little Milton
Gumbo Blues- Mitch Woods

Totally Q

The Gumbo Song- Bill "Sauce Boss" Wharton & the Ingredients
Ham Bone and Sweet- The Four Southern Singers
Have Myself a BBQ- Porterhouse Bob
Henpecked Daddy- Ralph Johnson
Hey Chef- Slim Gaillard
Hey Pete! Let's Eat More Meat! - Dizzy Gillespie
Home Cookin- Junior Walker
Hope To See You At My Bbq- Wheelerham
Hot Barbecue- John P. Gelinas
Hot Dog Buddy Buddy- Bill Haley
Hot Dogs & Cabbage"-Little Wally
Hot Pastrami-Joey Dee & The Starlighters
Hot Pork Sandwiches- Tanita Tikaram
Hot Sauce- Thomas Dolby
Hot Sauce- Bill "Sauce Boss" Wharton & the Ingredients
Hungry Man Blues- Nathan & The Zydeco Cha-Chas
Hungry Woman's Blues- Saffire-The Uppity Blues Women
I Crave My Pig Meat- Blind Boy Fuller
I Heard the Voice of a Pork Chop- Jim Jackson or Bogus Ben Covington
I Hear They Smoke The Barbecue- Hong Kong Stingray
I Like My Chicken Frying Size"-Merle Travis
I Love Bar-B-Q- Guy Brothers
I Love My Baby's BBQ- RJ's Rhythm Rockers
I Love My BBQ- Ted Nugent
Ice Cream Man - The Tornadoes
I'm a Hungry Man- Louis Jordan
I'm Cookin- Bill "Sauce Boss" Wharton & the Ingredients
I'm a Hog for You- Lynn August and the Hot August Knights
It Ain't the Meat- The Swallows
It's A Barbecue Tonight- Pan
I Want a Hot Dog for my Roll- Butterbeans & Susie
I Want Some Seafood, Mama- Fats Waller
Joey The Barbecue Blowie- Allan Caswell
Johnny Getting Out of Jail Barbeque- Liz Talley
Keep On Churnin' Til The Butter Comes- Wynonie Harris
Kidney Stew Blues- Eddie 'Cleanhead' Vinson
King of Barbecue- Gnu
Kingpin's Barbecue- Rusty Bladen
Korean Barbecue Blues- Andrew D. Gordon
Learned to Use the Grill Young- Dick Jumps

Totally Q

Let's Have a Barbecue- Matt Mattson
Little Red Rooster- Howlin Wolf
Live with the BBQ- Tom Trago
Living in a BBQ World- Drink Small
Livin' in a Drunken Barbecue Haze- Psycho Enhancer (this is music?)
Leons BBQ- Dave Nevling
Lower On the Hog- Mel McDaniel
Mama Bake a Pie (Daddy Kill a Chicken) -Tom T. Hall
Meat Cuttin' Blues- Hunter And Jenkins
Meat Eatin Man- Jerry Lee Lewis
Memphis Soul Stew- King Curtis
Memphis Women & Fried Chicken- Dan Penn
Mess Around- Dr. John
Mess Around-Ray Charles
Milk Cow Blues- Bob Wills
Minor's Barbecue- Felix Gross
Miss Bessies's Fine Bar B Q- Charlie Musselwhite
Miss Otis Regrets (She's Unable to Lunch Today) - Ella Fitzgerald
Mississippi Barbeque- Johnny Rawls
Miz Jacksons Fine BBQ- Charlie Burnett
Mommas Dance Hall Barbecue Barn- Brent Bennett and the Movers
Mommas In The Kitchen- Slim Gaillard
Mongolian Barbecue- Fermin Muguruza
Mr. Barbeque- Rickey Woodard
Mr. Green is the Barbecue Man- Drink Small
My Place BBQ- Diplomats of Sound
Neck Bones and Hot Sauce- L. Anderson & The Tarnadoes
Okra- Bill "Sauce Boss" Wharton & the Ingredients
Old People's BBQ- Barry Schwump (very short)
Old Pigweed- Mark Knopfler
Peace Love and BBQ- Marcia Ball
Pass the Biscuits Please- Jimmy Dean
Pat's Barbecue- The Lab Dogs
Pepper Sauce Mamma- Charlie Campbell and His Red Peppers
Pickin' A Chicken" - Eve Boswell
Pig Meat Blues- Georgia White
Pig Meat is What I Crave- Bo Carter
Pig Meat On The Line- Memphis Minnie
Pig Meat Strut- Big Bill Broonzy
Pig's Feet and Slaw- Tiny Parham And His Musicians

Totally Q

Pig Pig- The King Khan & BBQ Show
Poke Chop Sandwich- ZZ Top
Pork chops & Mustard greens-Ernie Andrews
Pork Chop Blues- The Two Charlies
Pork Store- The Booglerizers
Presbyterian Barbecue- Wal
Punk's Don't Have Barbecues- Red Zebra
Put Another Log on the Fire- Tom T Hall
Rawhide- Blues Brothers
Red Beans- Jimmy McGriff
Red Hot Chicken - Wet Willie
Red Neck BBQ- Big Ben Kennedy
Rev. Mccarty's Bbq Shack- Mingo Fishtrap
Ribs and Hot Sauce- Lionel Hampton & His Sextet
Ribs and Whiskey- Widespread Panic
Rib Shack Boogie- Steve Guyger and Big Joe Maher
Riffin At the Barbeque- King Coles Swingsters
Ring of Fire- Johnny Cash
Rock 'n' Roll BBQ- The Electric Boogie Dawgz
Rockin' At the Barbeque-Dave Fields
Round the Barbecue- Michel Schick
Rump Steak Serenade- Fats Waller
Salt Pork West Virginia- Louie Jordan
Saturday Night Fish Fry – Louie Jordan
Sam the hot dog man- Lil Johnson
Samba With Some Barbecue Sauce- Paul Desmond
Save The Bones For Henry Jones Cause Henry Don't Eat No Meat- Pointer Sisters
Schoolyard BBQ- Marcus Anthony
Scotty's Barbecue- Mannheim Steamroller
Selling My Pork Chops- Memphis Minnie
She's Got Sauce- G. Love & Special Sauce
Sheriff's Barbecue- Clarence "Gatemouth" Brown
Shortnin' Bread - Fats Waller
Sic em on a Chicken- Zac Brown Band
Smoke a Little Smoke- Eric Church
Smoke gets in your Eyes- The Platters
Smoked Meat Blues- Richard M Jones Jazz Wizards
Smokey Joe's Barbeque- Johnny Horton
Smokey Joe's Café- Buddy Holly
Smokin' In the Rockies -Sawyer Brown

Totally Q

Smokin With Some Barbecue- Kermit Ruffins and the Barbeque Swingers
Sparerib Rock- Barbecue Bob and the Spare Ribs
Solid Potato Salad- Nat King Cole
Southern Barbecue- Alligator Jackson
Stir Your Pot- Bill "Sauce Boss" Wharton & the Ingredients
Struttin with some Barbecue- Louis Armstrong
Stubb's BBQ- The Raj Pickens Soundsystem
Sunday Barbecue- Eddy Gober
Tailgate- Colt Ford
Take Out The Squeal (If you want a meal)- Earl Jackson
Task Force Bbq- Funk Shui
Texas Barbecue- Don't Ask
That chick's too young to fry -Louis Jordan
The Barbecue- Eddie Murphy (from his stand up bits)
The Barbecue- Diamonds in the Rough
The Barbecue Ghost and his Goal-Scoring Friend- Fitba Thatba
The Barbecue Song- The Guitarros Brothers
The Barbeque Ribs- The New Snot Nosed Bastids
The BBQ Song- Rhett & Link
The Big Butter and Egg Man- Kermit Ruffins and the Barbecue Swingers
The Christmas Family BBQ- Neil Andrews (OK, so there are two
BBQ Christmas songs)
The Chicken Song- Ernest Tubb & Red Foley
The Closer to the Bone (The Sweeter Is the Meat)- Louis Prima
The Tailgate Song- Nathan Osmond
They Don't Serve BBQ in Hell -Cary Swinney
Three Cord Barbecue- Jim Hoehn
Too Hot To BBQ- Brother Slade
Too Much Barbeque- Big Twist & The Mellow Fellows
Too Much Pork for Just One Fork- Southern Culture on the Skids
Tube Steak Boogie- ZZ Top
UFO's, Big Rigs and BBQ- Mojo Nixon
Uncle Joes Barbecue- The Mommyheads
Urban Barbecue- Chatos
Voodoo Barbecue- Monster Klub
Vegetarian Barbecue- De Portables
Wash my Spoon- Bill "Sauce Boss" Wharton & the Ingredients
West Coast Barbecue- Ramrod
What's on your Neighbors BBQ- Nekromantix
Who Did You Give My Barbecue To? Part 1- Big Boy Teddy Edwards

Totally Q

Who's gonna feed them hogs?- Tom T Hall
Who Stole the Hot Sauce?- Chubby Carrier
Wilke's BBQ- Bobby Watson
You Can't Hurry Ribs- (Meathead Goldwyn's theme song) Natalie Longo
You Can't Sell Barbecue- Snapp Tones
Your Greens Give Me the Blues- Rev. Billy C Wirtz
Zombie Apocalypse Barbecue- The Consortium of Genius

Index

Totally Q

Totally Q

Totally Q

Totally Q

Totally Q

Totally Q

Totally Q

Totally Q

CPSIA information can be obtained
at www.ICGtesting.com
Printed in the USA
FFOW03n0429250316
22594FF